The Rebel

and

Preacher Man

The True Love Story
of Russell and Susie Adams

Handwritten inscription:

4/18/2024

It is an honor to be a Missouri Baptist —
May God Continue the work He has begun in and thru you as you follow Him —

Susie K Adams
Psalm 117

Scripture Quotations taken from The Holy Bible:

King James Version – (KJV) public domain

English Standard Version (ESV) Copyright © 2001 by Crossway Bibles, a publishing ministry of Good News Publishers. Used by permission. All rights reserved.

Good News Translation (GNT) Good News Bible © American Bible Society 1966, 1971, 1976, 1992. Used with permission.

New American Standard Version (NASV) Copyright © 1960, 1962, 1963, 1968, 1971, 1972, 1973, 1975, 1977,1995 by THE LOCKMAN FOUNDATION A Corporation Not for Profit LA HABRA, CA All Rights Reserved

New King James Version (NKJV) Copyright © 1982 Thomas Nelson. Used by permission. All rights reserved

New International Version® NIV® Copyright © 1973, 1978, 1984, 2011 by Biblica, Inc.™ Used by permission of Zondervan. All rights reserved worldwide.

Revised Standard Version (RSV) Copyright 1952 [2nd edition, 1971] by the Division of Christian Education of the National Council of the Churches of Christ in the United States of America. Used by permission. All rights reserved.

The Living Bible (TLB) Copyright © 1971 by Tyndale House Foundation. Used by permission of Tyndale House Publishers, Carol Stream, Illinois 60188. All rights reserved.

All rights reserved

All rights reserved. No portion of this publication may be reproduced, stored in a retrieval system, or transmitted in any form or by any means—electronic, mechanical, photocopy, recording, or otherwise—without prior written permission of the copyright owner.

Published in the United States of America

Patches Joyland Press

Susie Kinslow Adams © 2023

Regina Albritton, Editor

Cover and Interior format by C.A. Simonson

ISBN: 978-0-9907700-5-3

DEDICATION

This book is dedicated to my four children: Laura Adams, Michael Adams, Debbie Cardwell, Ricky Hall, and their children and grandchildren. I am honored that you call me "Mom."

This story could not have been told without your unconditional love and support.

And to Russell who, by example, taught this rebel how to accept and share the love of Jesus in a whole new way. His steadfastness and his confidence in my call to write stretched my boundaries. I am eternally thankful.

Until we meet again...

Table of Contents

DEDICATION iii

ACKNOWLEDGMENTS ix

FOREWORD x

PREFACE xiii

1 - INTRODUCING THE CHARACTERS 15

2 - MY WAY OR THE HIGHWAY 23

3 - THE LURE OF TRAVEL... 26

4 - JOURNEY INTO THE FUTURE 30

5 - THEN THERE WERE THREE.. 34

6 - LIFE WAS NO BED OF ROSES 40

7 - THERE'S BEEN A CHANGE 46

8 - FACING WIDOWHOOD 49

9 - MOMMY AND ME 52

10 - TIME CHANGED EVERYTHING 56

11 - MY FIRST PASTORAL VISIT... 61

12 - GETTING TO KNOW THE PREACHER 64

13 - A THANKSGIVING DAY SURPRISE................................... 67

14 - FRIENDSHIP TAKES A TURN 70

15 - PREACHER MAN HAD A PLAN 73

16 - INTRODUCING ME TO THE CHURCH 76

17 - AS IF IT HAPPENED: THE REBEL UNDER PRESSURE 79

18 - BRIDE AND GROOM COUNSELING 83

19 - ABOUT OUR CHILDREN 86

20 - MOTHER'S TRADITIONAL CHRISTMAS BREAKFAST 89

21 - A CHRISTMAS LIKE NO OTHER....................................... 92

22 - OUR WEDDING IS WHEN? 96

23 - FEATHER FLOWERS AND LITTLE BROTHER'S ANXIETY 99

24 - OUR WEDDING 102

25 - PERFECT HONEYMOON DESTINATION.......................... 106

26 - FREE TO BE ME.. 110

27 - MRS. PREACH IN TRAINING 113

28 - HOW SWEET IT IS..116

29 - MEMORIAL DAY WITH OUR NEW FAMILY.............................. 120

30 - POKE GREENS AND BLACKBERRY BUSHES............................ 123

31 - MY STUBBORN WILL - GOD'S PATIENCE 125

32 - UNDERSTANDING MY NEW WORLD 128

33 - SAYING GOODBYE AND MOVING ON 131

34 - GOD BLESSES SUSIE'S FLOWERS 134

35 - WE' RE MOVING WHERE?... 138

36 - SOUTHERN CALIFORNIA HERE WE COME 141

37 - I WASN'T EXPECTING THIS 147

38 - PREACHER MAN – FOREVER LEARNING 151

39 - THE REBEL RETURNS 155

40 - HAPPY TRAVELERS ON THE ROAD AGAIN 158

41 - LIFT CLASS LESSON CONVICTS TEACHER............................ 162

42 - MINISTERING THROUGH CRAFTS 165

43 - ANSWERING GOD'S CALL 168

44 - FAMILY REUNITED 170

45 - FAIR PLAY MINISTRY 173

46 - WHERE THE BUFFALO ROAM 178

47 - COUNTRY LIVING AT ITS BEST.. 183

48 - PREACHER MAN ON THE LOOSE 189

49 - YIELDING TO GOD'S ULTIMATE PLAN 192

50 - WHAT HAPPENED TO OUR CALENDAR? 195

51 - SEEKING GOD'S DIRECTION IN MINISTRY............................. 199

52 - INSPIRING TIMES OF REFRESHING 204

53 - A NEW MOUNTAIN TO CLIMB 207

54 - SPEAKING OF MOUNTAINS 210

55 - SUSIE'S UNPLANNED FORTY DAY RESPITE 214

56 - RESPITE THOUGHTS FROM MY JOURNALS............................ 217

57 - PREACHER MAN PREPARES FOR A CHANGE 220

58 - MY ROMANTIC PREACHER MAN 225

59 - MORE THAN A BUMP IN THE ROAD 231

60 - A REASON FOR ALL THINGS 234

61 - PREACHER MAN'S HOMEGOING 237

62 - PERSONAL CHALLENGE FROM PASTOR RUSSELL ADAMS ..240

63 - AT LAST, MY FINAL THOUGHTS 243

REMEMBERING RUSSELL ADAMS 245

PASTORATES OF REV. RUSSELL A. ADAMS 249

ABOUT THE AUTHOR 251

THANK YOU..250

ACKNOWLEDGMENTS

The first honor goes to my Lord and Savior, Jesus Christ. Without Him in my life, this would be another story; one I would not choose to tell. I praise Him every single day for guiding my life.

Together Russell and I served Dallas County Southern Baptist Church as Director of Missions and Secretary for twenty one years. I continue to visit the churches on Sunday morning, they are my forever family. Their love, support and prayers keep me going. A special thanks to those who have prayed for God to guide each word as we began this book journey.

Thank you to those who read and reread all or part of my manuscript: Pam Eidson, Connie Derks, Pauline Lilley, Vicki Stafford, Cathy VanDruff, Ken McCune, and Steve Faxon. Apologies to any I left out. A special thanks to Pam, Connie and Steve for your bravery in asking, "are you really sure that is what you want to say?"

I owe a special gratitude to two creative geniuses who have been with me from page one. Regina Albritton and her family joined Harmony Heights Baptist Church two weeks after I married the pastor and we immediately became soulmates. We were asked to make posters for an area-wide event and she grabbed my hands and said, "we better pray first." She should get an award for the many hours she has poured over each chapter, forever correcting, suggesting, questioning.

C.A. Simonson, publisher assistant, is the easiest person I have ever worked with. She listens to my ideas and offers suggestions while keeping me on track. I am honored to have her publish my books for me.

C.A. Simonson helping Susie at Panera Bread

FOREWORD

Five years ago, Preacher Man and I knew God desired this book to be written. For three years we discussed what should and should not be included. We laughed. We cried. We shared stories. We prayed. And prayed. And prayed.

August 21, 2021, God called Russell home. One of his final instructions to me was "finish our story. Make sure the readers understand that God is the One who drew us together. Help people know and love our Jesus."

Russell and I knew beyond a shadow of a doubt that, from the first time I visited his church, God worked miracles in each of our lives. On a scale of one to one hundred, giving reasons we should marry, we would barely have scored ten. We knew God gave us a confidence and peace the world could not provide. Our union is a product of God's love in us and His Holy Spirit guiding us.

The most challenging part in writing our story has been in choosing which stories to tell. Volumes could be written of the lives we have seen changed completely as young and old yielded to God's tug on their hearts. Those stories are easy to tell.

More difficult to share are the dark spots, the bumps in the road. Russell and I agreed those must be told as well. God does not waste anything; He has used each situation to grow us as individuals and to use those experiences to help others along their way.

To this day, I weep when I realize God allowed me to be a pastor's wife, Bible teacher, women's leader forty plus years, and still going strong.

And, above all else, to be called "Mom" by four amazing children. It's a high calling, I do not take it lightly.

You can read the story with confidence knowing this author has prayed for you. I am asking God to reveal Himself fresh to you, dear reader, that you will come to know and understand the powerful love He has for you personally.

I am making a scrapbook of testimonies for our children and grandchildren. I want personal testimonies from those whose lives have been touched through our ministries in some way.

I want to hear from you.

Email: susie@susiekinslowadams.com

Website: www.susiekinslowadams.com

Mailing address: P.O. Box 138, Buffalo, MO 65622

The Rebel

and

Preacher Man

*The True Love Story
of Russell and Susie Adams*

Susie Kinslow Adams

PREFACE

The Rebel and Preacher Man is a true love story of how God drew a preacher in his fifties and an unchurched woman in her thirties together. It is a testimony of God's love shining through as He reveals Himself afresh in the life of Marcella, Russell's first wife, as she battles terminal cancer. Again, in the life of Bob, Susie's first husband, as he invites Jesus into his heart two weeks before his last breath. And, of Russell and Susie's forty-two-year journey which only God could have orchestrated.

> URBAN DICTIONARY: "Rebel - A person who does not conform to what others prefer."

THE YEAR IS 1926 -

- Calvin Coolidge is President of the United States.
- The United States launched its first fuel-rocket. It traveled forty feet.
- The first Pontiac was built; U.S. Route 66 from Chicago to Los Angeles was created.
- The Kelly Blue Book was established; National Broadcasting Company (NBC) is launched.
- The first SAT tests were administered.
- Henry Ford announced a forty-hour work week with wages raised to $5 a week.
- United States population was 115 million.
- **Sunday, June 27, 1926**:
  Russell Allen Adams was born in Garden City, Oklahoma.

THE YEAR IS 1942 -

- Franklin D. Roosevelt is President of the United States.
- WWII 1941-1945. U.S. and Philippines troops fight Battle of Bataan.
- The draft age was lowered from twenty-one to eighteen.
- Daylight Savings Time goes into effect in the U.S. on February 8.
- Coffee, and gas (three gallons per week) were rationed in the United States.
- Wages were forty cents per hour--$16 a week.
- U.S. population was 326 million.
- **Thursday, December 10, 1942:** Carrol Sue Kinslow was born in Wichita Falls, Texas.

ങ൙

1 - INTRODUCING THE CHARACTERS

"...yea I have loved thee with an everlasting love: therefore with loving-kindness have I drawn thee." Jeremiah 31:3 (KJV)

PREACHER MAN'S STORY – IN HIS OWN WORDS
(Information gleaned from his personal journal, family records, and ministry files)

Russell Allen Adams, born June 27, 1926, in Garden City, Oklahoma. Son of Hiram John and Mamie Laura St. John Adams. Youngest of ten children; oldest brother Clarence, born in 1900; oldest sister Mabel, born in 1902. (Siblings: Clarence, Mabel, Hazel, Elsie, Flossie, Eugene, Nellie, Ora, Lawrence).

I was raised in a very crowded four-room house on a twenty-acre truck farm near Bird Creek, in West Tulsa, Oklahoma. Chores included milking, feeding horses, pigs, and chickens, and working in the fields and vegetable gardens. We kids rode on a neighbor's running board to church as a child. My favorite toys were toy train, red wagon, and Chinese checkers. Christmas day was a day we did not work in the field and enjoyed the holiday. We kids could go to a church service where we eagerly received a bag of goodies. Hard candy and chocolate were a treat for us. Later we had gifts from friends at school and relatives. Our parents worked hard and could afford little extras. My parents wanted me to be honest and reliable in whatever I did. If I had a special talent as a child, it was my loud voice. I was asked to use it in some school activities. Favorite activities growing up were going to Farmer's Market in Tulsa, Oklahoma and getting a hamburger at a cafe on the way home. My favorite uncle was an itinerant preacher. We all looked forward to him coming to our house.

I met 26-year-old Marcella Rae Williams through a friend. We were married January 31, 1953. I went overseas three times in the army during World War II. I reached Sergeant First Class. It was exciting but I was glad to return to America. My greatest joy in being a father was watching my children as they grew and seeing them happy and successful in their lives. Also, hearing them give testimonies of God's goodness to them. I would describe success as preaching the Word of God and always being honest and faithful. The most enjoyable job I ever had was as pastor of my first church in 1963 for $20 a week, The one thing I would never change about the way I've lived my life is the plan of salvation. I know in whom I have believed. The one thing I wish I had done differently in my life is to become a Christian in early life. Also, to get more education and live a more committed life to Jesus Christ.

Russell with Laura and Michael

MARCELLA'S STORY – IN HER OWN WORDS

Russell, Marcella, Debbie, Michael, and Laura Adams

Russell's first wife, Marcella, had carefully typed her personal testimony about four months before God called her home. Whether you believe in literal angels or not, I do. I had never seen the papers before; if Russell knew about them, he never showed them to me. This aged two-page typed testimony was found underneath a stack of papers I had brought home from my Cousin Penny's house after she passed away.

There is no explanation except for the fact that God in His wisdom wanted Marcella's testimony included in this book. Not only do I praise Him, but when I finally get Home, Marcella Williams Adams is one of the first people I want to meet. For now, I want to honor her by printing her letter in our book, exactly as she typed it about one year after being diagnosed with terminal cancer.

"GOD'S PROMISE TO ME"

First of all, I was saved at a very early age during Vacation Bible School. I was not baptized until many years later. After my conversion I continued in church until my teen years and since my parents did not attend, I dropped out. Later in life I met and married my husband. We were not active in church for several years. Finally, we started attending church services and even became members. We both felt there was something missing here. so we were invited to a revival service in a small Baptist church. My husband was saved, and I rededicated my life. We were baptized along with thirty-one other people. I had now found my place of service for the Lord. There was plenty to do and thank God the church put us to work, because the Lord was preparing us for something greater yet. After about a year, my husband answered God's call to preach. Well, to make this a little shorter we moved to Missouri for him to attend college. And the year we were there I had an abdominal pregnancy and lost a little girl at seven months. The Lord saw us through this and six months later I returned to the hospital for another abdominal surgery. After this the Lord really began to bless my life. First he gave us Debbie who was ten. The next year he gave us Laura, who was four weeks old, and a precious bundle of joy. After a few years later, another precious jewel came. His name was Michael. God has given us a great privilege to lead all three of my children to Christ. During our ministry in Northwest Missouri, I returned to the doctor and found I had a blood sugar of 460. The Dr.'s. first words were "you should be in a coma." So I entered the hospital. My eyesight left me but God saw me through this without any eye damage. Now this should bring us to the present time. I had surgery last April 14th and found I have cancer and I was told I had six months to live. I accepted this because I have a promise from God that He is in control of our lives. It will be a year in April, and I'm still living one day at a time. These experiences have helped me to see that all of us have only a short time here, and we ought to make every day count for the Lord.

Debbie's wedding with Laura and Michael

We have God's promise in John 14 where Jesus said, "and if I go away, I will come again and receive you unto myself that where I am you may be also." He has given us the promise of life everlasting. Whether I'm healed in this life or the next, I'm in His hands. He promises never to leave us alone. Praise God for a life that is beyond this physical life."

SUSIE'S STORY—IN THE REBEL'S OWN WORDS

The Kinslow Family
Susie, Geneva, Frank, and Richard

Carrol Sue (Susie) Kinslow was born December 10, 1942, in Sheppard Field Army Camp in Wichita Falls, Texas, to Frank Clyde and Katie Geneva Kinslow. I had one brother, Richard Frank Kinslow born October 27, 1944.

Soon after I was born, my father left the army and moved our family to Ontario, California, where he and his brother, Murton Kinslow, operated several fruit markets. One year later, longing to be near their aging parents, my mother and dad gathered our few belongings and returned to Missouri. I think my love for trees and wildlife came naturally as we lived on forty acres near Grandpa Ambrose Kinslow's farm in Southwest City, Missouri.

Susie Kinslow Adams

Richard Frank Kinslow   - 1960 -   Carrol Sue Kinslow

My travel came to a halt when it was time to start school. My parents purchased twenty acres along busy 71 Highway at the edge of Goodman. My brother and I completed all twelve years of school at Goodman, both graduating with honors. Upon graduation, Richard joined the navy and furthered his education.

Working on the Newspaper staff:
Susie Kinslow, Co-Editor; Rachel Mayfield, Art Editor; Larry Ludiker, Sports Editor; Anne Nichols, Grade Editor; Mr. Williams, Sponsor; Barbara Price, Co-Editor

The rest of my story and that of my first husband, Bobby Lee Mabry, follows. And you will see how God clearly worked a miracle in our lives. And how God is the reason the marriage of *The Rebel and Preacher Man* became the "love story" we could never have predicted.

2 - MY WAY OR THE HIGHWAY

"Let every soul be subject unto the higher powers. For there is no power but of God: the powers that be are ordained of God."
Romans 13:1 (KJV)

September 1960

To this day, I can hear the clang of the iron bars slamming shut and me being locked in a tiny, smelly jail cell; seventeen years old, hundreds of miles from home, and totally broke.

"Young lady, you need to learn laws have to be obeyed by everyone. If I had my way, I would send you straight home." Not an ounce of compassion or concern showed in the jailer's stern voice. Not only that, but it was almost time for me to go back to the motel and I was getting hungry...were they going to feed me or let me starve?

Home? The thought of being sent home to my mother was more frightening than staying in jail. I could picture her now; her face red as her hair as she screamed "Why didn't you listen to me? You could have found a good job near home. You knew better than to head out across the country with a bunch of strangers!" Perhaps she should remember she met the "strangers" who were going to take me "across the country" and seemed to have approved of them.

* * *

Thinking back on my life, Mother and Dad influenced my desire to travel without even realizing it. By the time I was five years old, we moved at least four times. Mother often said my first words were, "I want to ride, and ride, and ride".

Along with the lure of travel was my love for people, all people. I was anxious to meet new students in school and hear

The Rebel and Preacher Man

their stories. I was involved in Glee Club, Pep Club, FBLA, FHA, and 4-H. Summers were filled with 4-H and church camps, and several Vacation Bible Schools.

Despite my rebellion from time to time, church was a significant part of my growing up. I accepted Jesus Christ as my Savior at age thirteen. I wanted to follow Him and eagerly attended every revival, church camp and Bible School–whatever denomination. I memorized scripture and recited Bible stories at every opportunity. (Telling stories was one of my favorite things to do...and still is to this day.)

Most of my graduation class of nine girls and nineteen boys grew up together. We were much like brothers and sisters in a big family, full of fun and mischief. I hesitate to admit it; I was often the instigator.

My rebel side came out one sunny day just after I was allowed to drive Mother's car to school. That was indeed a rare occasion, and I made the most of it by gathering a few friends to go to the creek after lunch. We were fully aware the principal was watching from the front steps – but not to be deterred, we loaded the car and headed out anyway. But there would be a price to pay!

The next morning, the principal had his say. For one entire week, we could not speak to each other in class or sit together in the lunchroom. Our classmates chattered all around us as we sat pouting at separate tables. It was the longest week ever! (I'm not telling what happened at home, but it was not good.)

Another time I handed out some of Dad's cigars to a school bus full of kids headed to an out-of-town basketball game. It sounded like a fun idea at the time – not fun later. When Dad discovered his cigars were missing, guess who met me at the front door just as I got home from school!

The thing is – a teenage girl needs some privacy and time to find her way. My family lived in a three-room house. Our only phone hung on the wall in the kitchen and was used mostly for Dad's work, certainly not for chatting endlessly with my friends. My brother and I each had a couch to sleep on in the living room. This meant I had to go to bed and to get up at the same time everyone else did. There was no "just me" space.

The rebel in me showed up again a few weeks after graduation. Knowing I could get a free education in the service and decide on a career, I set out to join the Navy. I felt there was no need to discuss this with Mom and Dad; so, I confidently entered the Joplin Naval Recruiting Office. I was ready and willing to sign up and set the world on fire! After a few preliminaries, my spirit was quickly dampened as I heard the words, "I'm sorry, Miss. You are five pounds over our maximum weight. You are welcome to come back and try again if you want."

Embarrassed, shocked, and crushed in spirit, I rebelled. I thought, "Five pounds? You have got to be kidding! That was probably the big lunch I ate on the way here. If you don't want me like I am, tough. It's your loss!"

Without giving it another thought, I purchased a Joplin Globe newspaper and stomped my way two miles across town to my Grandma Doke's house to find myself a good job. Searching the "Help Wanted" section of the paper, my countenance brightened… because there, right before my eyes, was the perfect solution.

TRAVEL THE UNITED STATES FOR FREE. ALL
EXPENSES PAID. CAR FURNISHED. FREE
TRAINING. NO EXPERIENCE NEEDED.

The ad had my name written all over it!

3 - THE LURE OF TRAVEL

"If I rise on the wings of the dawn, If I settle on the far side of the sea, even there your hand will guide me, your right hand will hold me fast."
Psalm 139:9-10 (NIV)

A week later Mother and I walked into the historic Keystone Hotel on Fourth and Main Streets in Joplin. I was overwhelmed with excitement and awe. Mother was cautiously anxious to meet the people I would be leaving town with. Many of her fears were relieved as we were greeted by a very pleasant young couple and their infant daughter. Both were more patient than I with Mother's endless questions. She loved me and had legitimate concerns about me taking off to who-knows-where with strangers.

At a time when traveling sales crews were all too often careless with the monies they collected and known to abuse their employees, God surely was watching over this country girl. Our managers, the Davis family, took extra measures to make sure all the money we collected was turned in and products were delivered in a timely manner.

An added plus was their personal care. We became a close-knit family. I felt safe in going to them with health issues or any questions or concerns. And, as much as possible, they kept the young guys and gals separated.

Our newly formed team left the next day for a beautiful lodge in Arkansas. There we could get acquainted and learn the ins and outs of door-to-door sales. I have no idea what I thought the job was, but door-to-door peddling magazines certainly was not it!

On the job, we were to pose as students raising money for college. We were told to choose a profession or area of study we were interested in and the school we hoped to attend. "You will have much better sales if you can get the customer to relate to you as a neighbor." I was already feeling weak-kneed as she continued, "This is a good line to make it happen: 'I live right outside of town; I'm sure you know my daddy, Rex. Everyone in town knows him.' This will come more naturally to you as we go."

Come more naturally? To lie about school and where I live? My mother would kill me if she knew what I was doing! I knew this was wrong; nevertheless, my stubbornness and the yearning to travel were beginning to win.

As I sat there struggling with my conscience, Mr. Davis spoke up. "By the way, do any of you know how to drive a stick shift? We need someone to drive one of our cars so my wife and I can ride together."

Drive a stick shift? I learned to drive on a stick shift! I was totally hooked. As we left the lodge and I climbed behind the wheel of the classy black and white '58 Chevy, I was overcome with joy. Now, this is living!

For the next several months I worked hard and excelled in sales. My heart hardened as it became easier to slip into the part of a local college girl. I was promoted to "Trainer" teaching new recruits how to have consistent sales.

We worked our way east through Kentucky and Tennessee then turned south through Georgia and Florida. Every state stirred my gypsy blood; I longed for more. I was enamored by the palm trees, sandy beaches, aroma of orange groves and the splash of the ocean waves.

Of course, I did miss my family, especially my mother and little brother. However, it was not a big issue until I faced the Christmas season in Daytona Beach, Florida. I missed the snow,

The Rebel and Preacher Man

the smell of cedar on the fire, and my family. No more door-to-door sales for me! I needed to go home, love on my family, and get a real job.

It was good to be home with family and friends; even my own bed on the couch was good. Mother was making plans for the two of us before my suitcases were unpacked. However, after a few weeks waiting on tables, the wanderlust returned. I seriously and briefly considered college, but it wouldn't have allowed much time for my roaming. As the new year rolled around, I rejoined the sales crew. Three months later I quit again, for good this time. I explained to the boss that door-to-door sales was not what I was cut out to do. This time I was sure my decision was the right one for me.

About the time I decided to move in with relatives in Kansas City and find work, Mrs. Davis called. "Sue, we really need you. You do not have to do sales ever, or even be involved in training. We know we can depend on you and we want to offer you a job taking care of our Lisa. You will be responsible for her while we work. We can pay you a good salary plus all expenses paid. We are in Alabama now and can send you a ticket right away."

The shocker of the call: Mother was even happy for me. "Carrol Sue, I know how much you miss traveling. Maybe this will be a good way for you to see the country and enjoy what you are doing. You know I will be praying for you and the little girl in your care."

Again, I found myself overjoyed. Not only did I not have to be in sales, but I had all day to find places for Lisa and me to spend our time: parks and playgrounds, shopping, local events, and historical sights. Lisa was a healthy, growing toddler and easy to please.

The team changed considerably in the few months I had been gone. There were several new young men and women for me to meet. One fella, Bob, was exceptionally friendly. He was handsome with his thick, curly blonde hair, blue eyes, and winning smile. He was a good salesman, often ending his route early and wasting no time in getting acquainted.

"You have to come to Virginia sometime," he'd say as he described the beauty of the Blue Ridge Mountains and all the lakes and streams. He painted a charming picture of his family and his mother's home across a swinging bridge. The stories he told of winter's challenges when the bridge was too iced over to cross stirred my roving spirit. Over the next few months, I fell in love with him and his family as he described them to me.

4 - JOURNEY INTO THE FUTURE

"Man proposes but God disposes." Proverbs 19:21 (TLB)

August 1961

Our crew was in Ohio in August when Bob and I decided to get married. Because I was only eighteen years old, I had to call home to get my parents' permission. Mom and Dad were not in favor, but they knew this rebel would wait until she was in a state where she could marry without parental consent. We married in August and didn't go home until December.

Bob and I were married seventeen years. I could write books about those years; bestsellers no doubt, if I were to tell the whole story. Enough needs told for you to understand God's amazing grace! Not only to me, but to Bob and his family as well.

What little I knew about the "birds and bees" I learned from a book Momma gave me. (By the way, the pictures were disgusting.) Bob was ten years older than me; had been on his own since early childhood and was very street-savvy. I remember being too embarrassed to change baby Lisa's diaper in front of him.

In the beginning, I was struck by his manners, his captivating smile, and his friendliness. Bob was extremely polite and respectful toward me. I never once heard him raise his voice or question anything I did or said. He was the perfect gentleman and loved by all who knew him.

But we didn't really know him. In a few short weeks of marriage, I came to realize he seemed to have multiple personalities. He had a knack of turning proper behavior on and off without warning. He grew up with no restrictions, no positive authority figures, and little sense of right and wrong. His parents were divorced and remarried. The few times we visited his dad and his dad's family, it seemed like visiting my own relatives. I always wished I could have spent more time getting acquainted with that side of his family.

His mother and many of her siblings were hard drinkers and vicious when crossed. I've seen cousins chase one another across the swinging bridge with guns. It seemed lies were told when the truth would have served better and physically pounding on anyone who crossed you was the norm.

Of course, I did not see all this right away. The first few years as newlyweds were good for the most part. We finally left the sales crew and moved to Joplin, Missouri to be near my family. Dad was eager to teach Bob how to finish sheetrock and remodel old homes. They worked extremely well together as long as they left the alcohol alone. That's a tale for another time.

Getting acquainted with my family was a culture shock for Bob. We naturally showed affection to one another by a lot of hugging. He was not used to our kind of affection and was suspicious and jealous of anyone who would hug on me. His family was so messed up in that way, it was extremely difficult for him to accept genuine love-hugs between aunts and uncles and cousins.

After taking a few courses at Joplin Business College, I got a good job with Fleming Foods (formerly IGA Grocers). I worked in the Accounting Department when their first computer was installed. Yes, installed! It wasn't shipped in a little box. This new monstrosity filled an enormous climate-controlled room and seemed to have a mind of its own. I recall spending hours searching for a penny error! Can you imagine our thoughts in the sixties after we were told computers would soon be in every home?

Eventually, we moved to North Kansas City and Bob got a good job in construction, I at Kraft Foods. The first two weeks of my job we were broke. Kraft gave everyone packages of all their new sauces which I used as gravy on our meager meal of biscuits. If you are hungry enough, a hot barbecue or hollandaise sauce biscuit is quite tasty! We regularly picked up pop bottles along the road, but the money went for his cigarettes.

Bob and our first home

The mid-sixties were some of our best years, as for the first time, we became homeowners. We purchased a small, one-bedroom trailer in North Kansas City and later moved it to a beautiful mobile home park in Gladstone, Missouri. There was a lot to see and do when we were not working, and we were both making a good income.

Bob never lost his penchant for cars; he traded cars often. With both of us earning a good paycheck, we were finally able to finance a new car. Imagine our pride as we pulled onto the highway in our brand new dark blue Ford Mustang with a white interior. Not surprisingly, he immediately wanted to visit his family in Virginia; most likely to show off his classy 1965 Mustang.

As we prepared for vacation, he repeated a conversation I heard many times before. "You need to know if we get to see little Ricky, we are bringing him home with us."

"Oh, sure," I said. "I know how much you love that little boy." I readily agreed to avoid any argument. I felt there was no reason for concern because no mother could ever let her young child go across the country to live with Bob and a woman he never met. There was no way that could ever happen.

Ricky at his home in Williamsburg, VA.

5 - THEN THERE WERE THREE

"Even a child makes himself known by his acts, by whether his conduct is pure and upright." Proverbs 20:11 (ESV)

As we drove through the beautiful Blue Ridge Mountains into the Roanoke-Salem area of Virginia, I was spellbound. In all my travels, I have never seen a more magnificent countryside. Bob seemed happy to remind me he told me so… "Didn't I tell you!" Bob's mother, Katherine and stepdad lived in a small house across a river in Salem. It was a beautiful place to live except during spring rains. If the river flooded the yard and rose into the house, there was no escape except to hike up the mountain ridge behind their house and wait for the waters to recede.

My heart raced rapidly the first time I navigated the wobbly swinging bridge with cracked board flooring to get to their house. I never did get comfortable crossing that bridge. The family and locals ran across the bridge as if it were a pathway on dry land. Not me.

As soon as we arrived, Katherine wasted no time telling Bob that Ricky should arrive soon from Williamsburg with his family. Bob never told me why he held such deep love and concern for Ricky. I knew Katherine kept him in her home for long periods of time. Perhaps Bob held that little baby in his arms, changed him, fed him, cuddled him, and grew to love him as his own. I don't know.

Whenever Bob mentioned taking him home with us, I smiled; still confident it could never happen. No one would ever send a precious child home with us--especially if they knew Bob.

I was so wrong, so very wrong. Not only did it happen, but

his mother let us take her little 10-year-old son to Kansas City, Missouri, without hesitation. We were told his new school clothes and personal belongings would be sent as soon as they returned home. After a few weeks, we received one small box containing his Bible and a few older clothes. There was no further contact from his family, so Ricky stayed with us, and we proudly raised him as our own.

Bob, Ricky, and Grandpa

Excitement filled our car as we headed for Joplin to introduce Ricky to his new grandparents. My mother and dad were overjoyed to welcome their new grandson into the family. It was truly love at first sight. Ricky's smile was broader than ever as he was hugged tightly by his very first grandparents.

Ricky was a handsome little dark-haired boy with brown eyes and an award-winning smile. His legal name was James David; he was nicknamed "Ricky" after Ricky Ricardo. True to his name, Ricky quickly won the hearts of everyone in our mobile home park; especially the ladies when he helped carry their laundry or groceries.

My brother, Richard, was in the Navy at the time. He was

overjoyed to meet his new nephew and brought him a huge battleship that took a dozen batteries to run. Most people assumed Ricky was so named after his Uncle Richard. I don't believe either of them minded that assumption at all.

The next year, we purchased a larger mobile home and moved it to a beautiful corner lot in the same park. Ricky helped me plant flowers around our little picket fence. It was a year of firsts for our son including his first room of his very own. He knew he was secure and had a family and friends who truly loved and cared for him.

Bob's urge to move periodically led us to Joplin in the late 1960s. For a little down, we bought a house by Junge Stadium in the southwest area of town. It was structurally sound but needed major work on the interior. The wainscoting around the dining room and living room walls had to be removed before we could hang new sheetrock, texture, and paint. The major challenge for me was to keep the kitchen clean enough to cook and serve meals throughout the renovation. Bob threw a fit if there was any dust or debris where he ate. Ricky was a big help in keeping things cleaned up and in order.

Susie and Ricky

My hopes of settling down in our beautiful home and Ricky finishing school in one place were in vain. As soon as we finished the house and gathered enough furnishings to make it pretty, Bob sold it. Completely furnished. Completely! We walked out of there with only essentials and our personal belongings. He was ready to move on, no questions asked.

Bob and Ricky

Ricky and I learned early on to not get too attached to where we lived or to the cars we drove. When Bob had decided the Mustang was not large enough for the three of us, he traded it for a classy baby blue 1962 Cadillac. On a cloudy day in March 1970, we crammed all we could into our "new" car and headed to Florida. Ricky and I never understood why we kept moving, but we both knew any discussion of the matter was out of the question.

As it happened, since we were going to leave Joplin, this was the perfect time. Lee George, the local weatherman predicted light snow flurries for the next day. He was following the national forecast for the region although he admittedly did not agree with it. Joplin got flurries all right – about twenty inches of them in a twenty-four-hour period. As we made our way to the warm sunny coast, our former home was buried in over twenty inches of snow. The area was paralyzed. Schools closed, telephone circuits jammed, and carports across town collapsed as tree branches fell from the weight of the snow.

In the years following, my heart ached for Ricky having to change schools at a minute's notice. However, I was not brave enough to stop the cycle we were in. The quiet, polite Bob that I married was indeed a wolf in sheep's clothing. He questioned everything I did and displayed a violent temper if he didn't get his way. In the sixties and seventies, there were few places to get help if you were in an abusive or compromising situation; you were on your own. All too often women were seen as the blame for problems in the home.

Ricky at Bob's gas station in Florida

After a year of roaming around, we returned to Missouri. Ricky and I were happy to be back around family. Mother, her sister Josie, and daughter Penny, each owned a home in Webb City. Bob was the perfect husband around them. He even encouraged me to spend time with them and go on outings. I was in hopes this was the final move for a while; everything seemed to be going extremely well.

We bought a house in town with a huge, detached garage. After working regular jobs for a while, we decided to turn our big garage into a warehouse for ongoing sales. We reclaimed and recycled old furniture before it was the thing to do. We also bought out rummage sales and hauled off people's unsold items. This kept our garage full of merchandise and our roving spirits intact—for a time.

I was sure this time we were set; I had family around me, and Ricky could finish school. One day our rummage sale was going well when, with no previous discussion, Bob introduced me to a customer. "Jim here is going to buy the house." The house? Our house was not for sale! I loved this place; I did not want to move again. My family was all here. What about Ricky? He was in his last year of school. Why now?

My questions went unanswered; there was to be no discussion. Bob sold it and in two weeks we loaded our eighteen-foot camper and truck and headed south. Cousin Penny and her husband Earl packed up and traveled along with us in their truck and camper.

Ricky moved twenty-seven times in the few years he was with us. Through it all, he remained the polite, helpful young man he always had been. This time he chose to get a job and

Ricky with Grandpa Kinslow

stay behind, first with my parents, later in an apartment of his own. He married and started a family while keeping the same job for over thirty years.

6 - LIFE WAS NO BED OF ROSES

"God is our refuge and strength, a very present help in trouble."
Psalm 46:1 (KJV)

During our years of marriage, some were very, very good years, others extremely hard and even dangerous. I'm finding it difficult to write this because it is embarrassing, painful, and surely it couldn't have happened to me! Oh, but it did, and so much more I will never tell.

Born and raised in Virginia, Bob loved music and often sneaked into brush arbor meetings as a small child to hear all the people singing. I was surprised at the lyrics he still remembered. His blue eyes sparkled, and his smile broadened as he sang: "*My God is real, real in my soul. My God is real, for He has washed and made me whole...*" And for a season, life was good.

If I dared to suggest we go to church, he let me know we did not need church. So, imagine my surprise when he announced one Sunday, he wanted us to go to church. He was working construction in Florida and his boss invited him to a little country church. My joy quickly turned to fear as we entered the sanctuary on Sunday. The pastor was publicly accusing his wife of an affair. We quickly left as a bitter fight ensued. Bob never darkened the door of a church again.

I was sincere when I asked Jesus into my heart as a young teen. I knew Jesus had forgiven me of my sins and changed my life completely. My desire was to help others come to know Him. Yet, I soon let the cares of the world and my stubborn will pull me aside. For too many years my life was anything but Christ-like. This truth I want to make crystal clear...I left God. He never, ever left me. In the times I was most fearful or timid, His Spirit was at work in my life. He never forced Himself on me, but I knew He was there.

If I had to describe our marriage, I would say it was a roller-coaster ride. When things were good, they were top-notch. We worked together to make our homes appealing, whether a tiny apartment or house, renting or buying. Bob was good at helping me keep things clean and in order. We both enjoyed working in the yard, garage sales, eating out, and traveling. His jobs varied from construction, door-to-door sales, delivery, farming, or store clerk. He operated a service station in Florida and did quite well. When he worked, he worked hard and did a good job until he got an urge to move on.

Dad called us gypsies because we didn't stay in one place like him and Mother. In the beginning, we continued to travel and sell books door-to-door for a few months, then settled in Virginia for the winter.

In the seventies, while working in accounting for a mobile home manufacturer in Salem, Virginia, I created small flower arrangements made from dyed turkey and goose feathers and colorful fake fur. They sold so well to the girls in the office, the boss ordered them for his mobile home showrooms across the state. With all his orders, I decided to quit office work and opened "Susie's Shelf" on Main Street.

At night Bob drove me to area florist shops so I could sketch the arrangements in their window displays. The local Ben Franklin store was my supplier of colored feathers. For fifty-nine cents I purchased a package of feathers in a variety of colors. One day a lady walked into my shop, handed me a note, and left. I never saw her again, but I know Who sent her. The note read; "Honey, your flowers are beautiful, but you need help.

"SUSIE'S SHELF," a new shop next to Eagle Stores on Main Street, opened recently. Susie Mabry, above displays an "iris" she crafted from special materials she orders. All her "flowers" are handmade by Susie herself, and they come in colorful arrangements she prepares or are sold individually for do-it-yourself flower-arrangers. Susie also creates toys and novelties for children, special gifts, small "birds," witches for Halloween, and decorative table pieces made to order. Register Photo/Pat Hooker

Hollywood Fancy Feather Company sells died feathers for six dollars a pound, any color." She was so right!

And, God is good, all the time!

Traveling in our campers with Penny and Earl led to new adventures. We spent an entire year working odd jobs from Virginia, down the coast into Florida and around the Gulf, spending weeks on Padre Island before ending up in Phoenix for the winter. On the coast, Penny and I made and sold feather/fur flowers and magnets to provide the guys with fishing money. And we consumed our share of delicious fish dinners.

Bob and I spent one winter in our eighteen-foot trailer parked behind a barn in Louisiana. We both were happy there although I was alone until he got home from work. (Too bad I wasn't writing at the time.)

In 1976, finally back in Missouri, we opened another flower shop. Paying eighteen dollars a month for our two-bedroom apartment seemed outrageous. However, after we textured and painted the walls and recovered the furniture, it was quite the showroom. Of course, we added a full array of my colorful flowers and plants. Whenever working on a project together, that he wanted to do, we made a good team and had lots of fun.

***

Duenweg, Missouri: When school closed for Christmas break, Ricky asked permission to bring his classroom Christmas tree home because we couldn't afford a tree. He and I decorated the tree with strung popcorn and red bows and enjoyed the holiday.

Joplin, Missouri: Ricky went by bus to visit Bob's mother in Virginia for a couple of weeks. He returned to find we painted and fixed up a big bedroom for him. In addition to his new room, Ricky recalls being excited because I hung the finch cage over the sink so the tiny bird could see out the window.

Penny and Earl were with us again in Corpus Christi, Texas, right after hurricane Celia passed through. With only a few dollars, we bought a big house and furnished it with odd furniture pieces and fabrics from the salvage yards and thrift stores. We turned it into a real showplace. Of course, we didn't stay there long.

It is difficult to put into words what I want to say next. Often my life seemed unbearable with no way out. In the sixties women were made to believe if there was a problem in their marriage, it was their fault. Going home was not an option. I feared my family getting hurt if I left. So, I treasured the good times and endured the bad. I'm thankful God instilled in me the ability to adjust and not hold things inside. I didn't understand and had no remedy, but I could not hate. I was sorry for what our son endured; but I must say it was nice to have Ricky in the family. I wished I knew how to help Bob become more stable. When he was good, he was so very good, and when he was bad....

With much prayer, I offer this small peek into the shady side of my world with Bob in hopes you will better understand God's amazing grace and love for His children.

In the years being married to Bob, many nights were spent being questioned about a perceived wrong on my part. In time, I understood this usually happened to take the focus off his own wrongdoings.

I have been kicked with boots, pounded upon, had knives thrown at me, hit with more things than I care to say, and clothing ripped off me because he didn't like what I was wearing. I got meaningless phone calls from him while at work; most likely to make sure I was actually there. I've been spied on, lied to, and lied about.

In Missouri, Bob and his brother had a vicious fight. Ricky and I quickly left and took refuge under the front porch all night to protect ourselves until the squabble was over.

On another occasion while living in Virginia, he phoned Mother in Missouri asking if I called her. He told her he lost me in the shopping mall and figured I might call home. He had not lost me; I temporarily fled from his violence.

When Bob got angry at anyone, there was no limit to the destruction he could do. One uncle dared argue back and Bob threw a lawnmower through the uncle's car windshield.

More than once when he tripped and fell when drunk, I sat on him until he passed out. He was always "sorry" the next day and went months with no recurrence.

One night he pulled the sun visor off and hit me while I was driving. I saw a patrol car in my rear-view mirror, so I began swerving and we were pulled over. He spent the night in jail and, of course, was the perfect husband for quite a while after.

Then after months of calm family life, he came in from work one night singing joyfully at the top of his lungs. He had been drinking again and was loaded. Coming inside the door, he accidentally knocked a planter to the floor. As it crashed, he immediately went into a rage and pulled a sink from the wall and began to wreck everything in sight. Ricky and I quickly exited and spent the night in the neighbor's shed. We could hear his car drive up and down the alley searching for us. Of course, when we returned the next morning, all was well, everything was cleaned up, and he was so, so sorry. And life was peachy keen for months after that episode.

7 - THERE'S BEEN A CHANGE

"Therefore if any man be in Christ, he is a new creature: old things are passed away; behold, all things are become new."
2 Corinthians 5:17 (KJV)

August 1978

In the late seventies, we settled in Joplin, Missouri, and bought a small home for fifty dollars down and fifty dollars a month to remodel. At the time, we were working for a contractor finishing old houses, so we had all the equipment we needed to do the work. And, for the first time in a long time, we enjoyed a steady income.

Life was going well; we were healthy, happy, and employed. We worked hard all week and on Sundays we took the Joplin Globe to Mother's for biscuits and gravy and hot coffee.

As I said earlier, Bob really enjoyed trading cars. I knew not to get attached to a particular vehicle because he wouldn't keep it long. He would tell me the engine or the transmission or something major was about to go out and we needed to trade. His favorite car lot at the time was Virgil Burtrums' on Seventh Street in Joplin. I was amazed when he kept going back to the same dealership because, without exception, no one ever left Virgil's sales lot without him sharing the Good News of Jesus. He was extremely bold in his witnessing, so much so I feared Bob would get angry. He never did.

It was a warm August evening when we stopped by Virgil's house to make the final payment on a vehicle. Virgil visited with both of us for quite a while on his front porch. As the conversation began to wind down, Virgil got serious. "Bob," he said, "don't you think it's about time you accepted Jesus Christ as your Savior?"

"Yes, Virgil, I do. I have been thinking about what you have said for a long time." The tone of Bob's voice seemed to be sincere.

He bowed his head as Virgil led him in a prayer. I was shocked. I found it difficult to believe Bob was serious. I thought maybe this was his way of putting the request to rest. We didn't discuss the conversation on the way home or later. He never talked about the decision. He did not have to say anything; there had clearly been a change in him from the inside out.

"You will be enjoying the sun porch this fall as you watch the leaves turn and the squirrels scamper for food. What color do you want it painted?" He ignored my comment that we both would enjoy it, and asked again what color I wanted him to paint it.

By the next week I knew from his actions that he was definitely sincere when he prayed with Virgil. I began to think perhaps we could get back to church, maybe he could sing in the choir, and I might do nursery or kitchen work. (Those who know me will quickly tell you, those are the two places I don't belong.)

Every day Bob seemed to be happier and more content than I had seen him in seventeen years. His conversation changed dramatically. He showed more compassion and concern for me, our home, and our family. Many times, throughout the day, he told me I was a good wife. "You have put up with a lot with me," he said.

In the past, he made a point to tell me he did not want me to get another man if anything happened to him. His thoughts had always been so self-centered. Imagine my surprise when he said, "If anything ever happens to me, I want you to get you someone

The Rebel and Preacher Man

who will do all the things you have been wanting us to do. Make sure he is good to you; you deserve a good man."

During this time, we were remodeling a two-story house in Carthage, Missouri. It was a big job. When we finished scraping and painting the outside, we were to go inside and repair sheetrock, hang wallpaper, and paint.

Bob felt tired on Monday so I finished what I could by myself. When I got home, he wanted to know how my day had gone. He apologized over and over for sending me to work by myself. I do not recall any other time in seventeen years that he apologized to me—unless there was something he wanted. He had called all our family while I was at work and suggested they come over for a visit after supper that night. He told me we needed to spend more time with our great family.

The next day, he was feeling better, and we headed to Carthage to finish the job. He was in an exceptionally good mood as he scraped the windows above the porch roof. Teasing me, he grinned as he climbed down the ladder. Just as he stepped to the ground, he suddenly grabbed hold of a nearby clothesline pole and without further warning, passed out.

The neighbor called an ambulance, which took an eternity to get there because they went to the wrong address. Bob never regained consciousness on the trip to the hospital. I called Mother immediately; we waited together an hour before we were informed he was gone.

Bob died two weeks to the day after Virgil led him to faith in Jesus Christ. His decision had been genuine; it clearly changed his life. By God's grace, it also changed his eternal destination.

This was two days before our planned surprise party for his 44th birthday on August 10.

8 - FACING WIDOWHOOD

"Do not boast about tomorrow, for you do not know what a day may bring."
Proverbs 27:1 (ESV)

Reality set in early when our son, Ricky, gingerly hopped out of his car with a birthday gift for his dad. "Mom, look at what I found. It's perfect for Dad, he is going to love it!" Immediately the color drained from his face. "Dad died? When? How? What happened?"

Without notice, our lives changed drastically. The fact of his sudden death was difficult to believe. He had not been ill recently or complained of any pain or discomfort. In a flash, the joy and excitement of planning a big surprise party was replaced with the overwhelming need to make final arrangements for our loved one's funeral.

Ricky bore the task of telling his young family Dad/Grandpa was gone. At the same time, I'm sure Mother was remembering the time two years prior that she found herself a widow when Dad had taken his own life, and she was left in shock to face many of the same decisions she was now helping me deal with.

With no discussion, Mother immediately packed up a few of my things and took me home with her. She was keenly aware I was in no shape to be alone. Mother knew Bob and I never made end-of-life plans, either physically or financially. I welcomed her help, calm spirit, and expertise.

Relatives and friends brought a week's worth of food and often came to comfort. I want to mention Uncle Mick and Aunt Allie Arnold's most practical gift because we've copied it many times. Instead of perishable foods, they brought disposables: paper towels, toilet paper, Kleenex, storage, and trash bags.

Included were coffee, creamer, sugar, drink mixes, and canned meats, breads, and crackers for us to nibble on.

To this day, I cannot recall which preacher did the funeral or his church affiliation. I do remember his words brought comfort and peace to my soul as he spoke of Jesus' love and forgiveness to all. I knew beyond a shadow of doubt my ornery Bob was finally at peace. I did not realize it fully at the time, but I believe God renewed my faith and gave me a new hope and direction.

Within two weeks, I loaded my old Chevy truck with ladders and equipment and bravely headed to Carthage to finish our job. My task was to repair sheetrock, paint, and hang wallpaper. Thankfully, Dad taught both my brother and I how to spot nails, texture, and paint at a young age.

Hanging wallpaper was another story! Dad never hung a strip of wallpaper in his life and neither had Bob. After my dad died, a realtor hired Bob and me to repair and paint the interior and exterior of a small house. He said he could hire someone to hang wallpaper in at least one room. Bob quickly replied, "Oh, Susie can do it for you. She does a fantastic job!" The realtor was elated. Susie was devastated. Not only had I never hung a piece of wallpaper in my life, but I never watched anyone hang it. (Remember, this was before all the handy How-To-Technologies we now have.) At the time, I still feared saying "no" to Bob. I immediately began visiting every paint store in Joplin and Carthage. I listened to filmstrips, read directions, compared what was said about the best wallpaper tools and adhesives. Now I could be called a professional wallpaper hanger.

Truthfully, it was a bit scary to go back to the job alone. Bob was not there to clean the brushes at day's end, make decisions on what equipment was needed, or steady the ladder for me in difficult places. I would have to load and unload all the ladders, equipment and supplies without his help.

One of the first contractors I worked for by myself gave me a Living Bible. He let me know he and his wife and children were praying for me and our families as we healed and adjusted to life without Bob. The last Bible I read as a teen was the King James Version of the Bible.

Regardless of what else was happening during the day, I became consumed at night by Christian radio and reading God's Word. My hungry soul soaked up every word I read. While the Living Bible was easy for me to read and understand, I often wished I had my old Bible to refresh my memory of verses I learned as a child.

Well into the night I stretched out on the floor with Bible in hand and the radio on. One program was "Night Sounds" which seemed to calm my spirit. My favorite at midnight was "Haven of Rest." *"I've anchored my soul, in the Haven of Rest, I'll sail the wide seas no more..."* I could never have imagined the future God was preparing me for as I slowly turned over every aspect of me to my Creator God.

I do know He took away all my fears and worries and guilt of the past. He restored my soul and gave me a hunger for Him. Without a doubt, I experienced the "peace of God, which passeth all understanding." Philippians 4:7 (ASV)

Through all of this, God had prepared a way for my precious mother and I to be together again.

9 - MOMMY AND ME

"As one whom his mother comforts, So I will comfort you; And you shall be comforted in Jerusalem." Isaiah 66:13 (NKJV)

Katie Geneva Kinslow, my mother and best friend for life, instilled in me a love for all God's creatures great and small. Together we enjoyed eating out, weekend excursions, visiting relatives and friends, crafts, artwork, painting, writing, and meeting new people; the list was endless.

Like all good friends, we had our moments. I grew up at a time when we did not question our elders, especially parents, at least

Susie and her mother

not in their hearing. I thought she dealt more harshly with me than with my little brother which made it difficult at times to get along with her. She was not careful with her words when she was angry! Of course, this young rebel resented not having the option to question what I was told to do.

In my eyes, she favored my brother, Richard. I'm sure I hold part of the blame as I could be quite stubborn and independent. I did not know until after I left home that mother had lost two babies at childbirth. Richard was born with serious health concerns and little hope of survival, plus we lived far from medical help or close friends and relatives. The struggles she had to cope with were unimaginable.

My dad worked hard in construction, painting and remodeling older homes. When his brother, Amos, returned to Missouri from California, he taught Dad how to finish sheetrock and add beautiful textured patterns to the walls. Being a new skill in southwest Missouri, they kept busy and made good money. Before long, however, Dad's drinking got the better of him and people took advantage of his failing health.

We were a typical 1950s family. Work, school, and caring for elderly parents consumed most of our time. Mother worked long hours in a laundromat (complete with wringer washers), and later as head cook in a fine restaurant. She always made time to prepare delicious meals for her family and support PTA and our school functions. She was also very active in community affairs trying to get a city park built, leading a local 4-H club, and even learned to play basketball with other ladies.

Mother owned a small, comfortable home and a nice car with few additional expenses. At a sassy sixty-four, she looked and acted more like fifty. A natural redhead with a beautiful smile and few wrinkles, she worked to maintain good health and mobility.

Widowhood and my flexible work schedule opened an exciting new world for us. Without any discussion, Mother immediately began to change her schedule so I could join her when possible. She began with her tole painting and exercise classes. I relished being able to spend more time together. I loved my mother and regretted the many years we were separated.

One of my favorite memories is time spent crafting at her big dining table. Whenever I had long periods of time between jobs, we created beautiful flowers from feathers and fake fur. Mother chattered on and on about the olden days and how they found a use for everything. I learned more about her childhood in that comfortable setting than she normally shared. Mother's life had been hard; beginning in childhood when she took care of her mother. Later she helped take care of her sister, Josephine, when she received third degree burns from a kerosene stove.

Once a week we loaded dozens of beautiful arrangements into the car and headed out to make our fortune. We knew every small Walmart store within a hundred miles. If their store didn't have a flower department, we were allowed to set our tables outside by the exit doors. Our flowers were colorful, inexpensive, and sold well.

Daily life began to take new directions as we realized our freedom to make our own plans. "Momma, I should finish the job I'm on tomorrow. Want me to take a few days off so we can have a little outing?"

I knew Mother was always ready and willing to go at a moment's notice; she kept her suitcases handy. (As I said earlier, I came by my traveling naturally.) "Sure, Honey. When can we leave? Are we going to Branson?"

As a true lover of nature, Branson was Mom's favorite go-to-place when I was in high school. The Baldnobbers, Sons of the Pioneers, Shepherd of the Hills, and Silver Dollar City were a few of the attractions which

Penny and Josie, Mom and Susie

opened in the fifties and sixties. I now realized what a loss it was for her when I left home after high school to traipse across the country. My dad rarely took Mother to a cafe for dinner. He was not about to spend the day driving around the country "playing tourist."

Aunt Josie, Mom, Cousin Penny, and Susie

"Sure, Momma, anywhere you want to go. Let's stay two or three days. We'll do Branson one day and Silver Dollar City the next. You can ask Aunt Josie and Cousin Penny to join us. I'll come get you early."

10 - TIME CHANGED EVERYTHING

"..not forsaking the assembling of ourselves together, as is the manner of some, but exhorting one another, and so much the more as you see the Day approaching." Hebrews 10:25 (KJV)

The hillsides were ablaze with crafts, foods, and musicians as the four of us munched on gooey funnel cakes. A day in Branson's Silver Dollar City quickly became our favored activity. Less than a two hour's drive away, inexpensive, and one location for a variety of activities.

Nearing time to head home, we joined the "congregation" in the Old Country Church one more time before getting our favorite snack. We gave little thought to the hard, rough benches as the pianist/song leader began pounding those ivories.

"Amazing grace, how sweet the sound. That saved a wretch like me. I once was lost..." We were quite the quartet as we belted out those old familiar hymns.

Our hungry souls seemed to beg for more. Not one of us was faithfully attending church although each professed to be a Christian. Finding a church home was a mere fleeting thought in my mind, but not so in Mother's. More than once in the next few days she suggested we go to church on Sunday.

"Sure, Mom. That's a good idea. We'll visit a few churches next month." Thoughts of entering a church building where I knew no one terrified me although crowds of strangers at the mall were not a problem. I knew she was right, we needed to be in church.

"Okay, Carrol Sue, don't forget what you said. We will start going to church in October." Oh, dear! She used my whole name; this was clearly more than a suggestion!

My phone rang early the next Sunday, the very next Sunday. "Good morning, Honey. It's a beautiful Sunday morning. Are you getting ready for church? The big one on seventh and Range Line has church service at 10:45. We don't have to go to Sunday School until we find a church we're comfortable in."

Thankfully, before I could insist we wait until October, she hung up the phone. God was gently drawing His wayward sheep back into the fold. I grumbled as I glanced at the calendar. Oops! What do you know - it was October. The first day of October 1978 was on Sunday! Me thinks God has a sense of humor.

Forest Park Baptist Church was a friendly church with heartfelt music from the choir and congregation. My hungry soul was nourished by the pastor's simple message of love and hope. We enjoyed a hearty lunch at a nearby buffet and decided next week we could visit a smaller congregation.

I was amazed, regardless of the size of the church, God seemed to speak directly to my soul. I never questioned where we went; we were asking God to direct us to His choice. But I stepped back a bit at Mother's latest suggestion: "Susie, I saw Harmony Heights Baptist advertised in the newspaper this week. It's only a few blocks from your house." Before I could answer, she added, "And they have a Single Adult Department!"

"MOTHER! Oh, gee, Mother! I will visit them with you next Sunday, but I WILL NOT go to any Single Adult class! The last thing I want, or need is some guy asking me to go out!"

She smiled and said: "I'll be at your house early. I feel good about visiting closer to your home. There is something about this one that simply feels right."

October 29, 1978

Would you believe...Sunday happened to be the first day of Daylight Savings time! (Godly humor again?) I am positive I turned my living room clock back on Saturday. Absolutely sure! I am also sure my dear mother moved it ahead while I was finishing up in the kitchen.

What a shock when we arrived in time for Sunday School and were led to the Single Adult class. Mother! Mother! Mother! I had heard about Singles' groups and seriously expected a bunch of guys looking over the two new 'prospects' during class. To my surprise, gals outnumbered guys about six to one. We were met with cheerful smiles, hot coffee, and doughnuts! I immediately recognized a couple of the women. One was Head Nurse on the night shift at the same time I worked as Secretary to the Director of Nursing at Freeman Hospital.

Mother was pleased when the entire class headed to the front of the sanctuary for worship; me, not so much! I would have chosen an obscure pew at the back of the sanctuary, near the door for a speedy retreat. Once a rebel, always a rebel.

The small, enthusiastic choir certainly prepared our hearts for worship. Our class and the friendly congregation made sure we felt welcome and invited us to come back for evening worship or the next Sunday. Although the Lord was clearly working on my heart and soul, I was not ready to make a commitment to be in the same church every week.

My mother, in true colors, commented on the way home. "I really liked hearing the pastor's message this morning. He sure is handsome! Someone in our class mentioned he was single."

Not only did I not hear the conversation about his being single, but I also really didn't care. What I did hear from his message was that he was passionate about telling others about Jesus' love for every person.

When in Joplin, Mother often spent time at my house between her various appointments in town. This Monday she waited for me to get home from work to tell me I missed a visitor.

"Susie, Pastor Adams was here earlier to visit. I do wish you had been home. He is really a very nice preacher and so easy to talk with and he liked your records. He has two little kids at home and a married daughter. I told him a little about our family and how you were working so hard. He mentioned to me about their Singles' Thanksgiving Dinner coming up November 23rd."

I was prepared to jump in when she paused to catch her breath. It didn't happen. She continued talking about that preacher. "Susie, he's such a good man. It's too bad he is too young for me and too old for you! He seems to care so much about everyone."

"What? What did you say? Seriously, Mother, the last thing in the world I want is another man. No, Mother, no! Not in this lifetime. Mercy, no! And, if I were to consider getting married again, it most certainly would not be to a preacher!"

Wanting to quickly change the subject, I continued. "There are several other churches in town we should check out before we make a decision."

Our search for a church we both liked continued into November. Momma obviously enjoyed Harmony Heights Baptist better than any others. Actually, I didn't want to admit it, but I did enjoy the Single Adult class. It was Thanksgiving week when we headed back to Harmony Heights for Sunday School and church. We were both ready for new friendships and eagerly returned for the evening services.

The Rebel and Preacher Man

Spotting us in class, Pastor Adams quickly approached us with a sign-up sheet for the Singles' Thanksgiving Dinner to be held in the parsonage. My response was quick, and firm. "We're not sure what we are doing Thanksgiving," Being in church was one thing, but I was not ready for a single's social event.

"You should come. You will enjoy the meal and getting acquainted. I am putting both your names on the list. We will be expecting to see you there." This Pastor Adams was sure persistent.

Of course, my sweet mother was all smiles while I tried my best to change the conversation. I did not need to get acquainted with everyone, I had plenty of good food at home, and had no intention of going to his house on Thanksgiving. My mind was made up, end of discussion!

Or was it?

11 - MY FIRST PASTORAL VISIT

"For thus says the Lord God: Behold, I, I myself will search for my sheep and will seek them out." Ezekiel 34:11 (ESV)

November 1978

My plans for Thanksgiving week were coming along nicely. Since I had no immediate work scheduled, I could catch up on household chores and prepare healthy meals to put in my freezer. Several local restaurants were advertising great Thanksgiving specials Mom and I could check out.

After enjoying a light breakfast, I opened the doors and windows to let the fresh autumn breeze flow through the house. Later, I would add fresh vegetables to a left-over roast for supper.

Thoughts of yesterday's soul-stirring messages and the good music at church continued to lift my weary soul. Suddenly, I remembered it was on a Monday when Pastor Adams visited Mother here while I was at work.

We applauded his passion for meeting people and boldly sharing Jesus with them. Perhaps he always visits on Monday. I should make my stew now in case he comes at lunchtime. (Note: If you ever questioned God's ability to direct one's thoughts, here is proof: Entertaining in any form has never been my forte' – especially cooking a meal for a preacher I hardly knew.)

With the roast warming on the stove, and a fresh pot of coffee brewing, I began peeling vegetables. *"There is sunshine in my soul today...."* My heart was truly happy for the first time in a long time. My singing was interrupted by someone at the door.

"Susie, are you home?"

"Sure, I'm in the kitchen. Let me dry my hands and I'll be right with you."

The Rebel and Preacher Man

By the time I got the towel from the rack, Pastor Adams had walked in and made himself at home at my kitchen table. "Don't let me interrupt your work. I had a wonderful visit with your mother a while back and wanted to get acquainted with you. I'm glad you both came back yesterday and stayed for all the services."

He continued to talk non-stop about Harmony Heights Baptist Church and the Singles' Department while I finished peeling the carrots and potatoes and putting them into the pot to cook.

"Let's go into the living room where it's more comfortable." I was thoroughly enjoying his visit and certainly did not want him to feel like he needed to leave.

To this day I can remember how peace flooded my soul as Mother and I began our search for a church to attend. I know now God was calling His children back into His arms.

There was something different about this man that had nothing to do with his profession. The composure I had talking with him that day surely came from God. Even as a child, I never wanted much to do with preachers; they made me nervous. As a young teen, I loved Jesus and wanted to follow Him. However, it seemed I could be good for only so long, then the rebel in me stretched the boundaries and I would mess up.

My brother and I attended every Bible School and camp in the area. I liked Bible Schools. I thought they were good especially because the preacher didn't come to our classes often. Of course, there was one day a week when he preached to us, and it always seemed to be directed right at me.

Camps were another story altogether. Being away from home a whole week with our friends was my best memory. However, there was preaching every day and again it seemed the preachers aimed their messages right at me! I was sure of it.

God worked in my heart through those long nights with my Living Bible and radio preachers. I knew it was my rebellious spirit that drew me away from hearing the gospel message the preachers were trying to tell me. I never liked preachers! I felt convicted, and rightly so.

"Do you have time to stay for lunch? I think the stew is ready."

We continued to chatter through lunch and into the afternoon. In many ways, I felt strangely like we were old friends getting reacquainted.

All too soon it was time for him to pick up his kids from school. We barely knew each other, but there was a peace in my heart after he left that I could not explain.

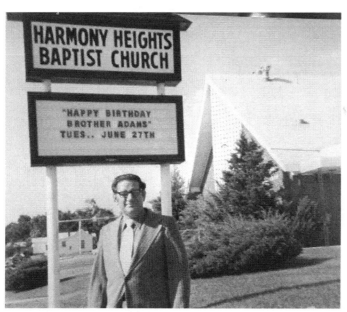

Note of Interest:

Harmony Heights Baptist Church in Joplin, Missouri was completely destroyed in the 2011 Joplin tornado.

Pastor Adams in front of Harmony Heights Baptist Church

12 - GETTING TO KNOW THE PREACHER

."...and the peace of God, which surpasses all understanding, will guard your hearts and minds through Christ Jesus."
Philippians 4:7 (NKJV)

My phone rang early Tuesday morning. "Good morning, Susie. This is Brother Adams. Are you free this afternoon? I'd enjoy hearing some of your good records before Mike and Laura get home."

With no immediate jobs scheduled, I welcomed the company. At this point I never gave much thought to his being a preacher, or a single guy for that matter. I was thankful to have a friend to share my music with.

It was perfect that he wanted to come in the afternoon since Mother and I made plans for the morning. "Sure, I'll have a pot of coffee brewing. Any time after one o'clock will be fine."

Mother and I shopped all morning before enjoying a leisurely lunch at Bonanza Steak House. It seemed she kept bringing the conversation back to "that nice Pastor Adams," which caused me to wonder what she was thinking. Not that it really mattered. I mean, he was simply being friendly to newcomers at his church.

Back home, I barely got the car unloaded and groceries put away when Russell arrived with a bag of cinnamon rolls to go with our coffee. There was no way I could tell him I was stuffed from a big lunch.

The afternoon went all too fast as we chatted over coffee with gospel music blaring in the background. He was seriously engrossed in the music, especially the older hymns. For the first time in a long time, I felt relaxed and was enjoying the moment.

Later I headed to Mother's to work on craft projects and enjoy her yummy potato soup and cornbread. She was full of chatter as usual. "I'm glad we are going to the Singles' Dinner at the pastor's house Thursday. He sure is a likable person. I do wish he was a bit older—or, younger."

I saw no reason to tell her about the preacher and me spending so much time together. After all, it was a simple friendship, and that was all it could ever be.

Russell called later that night to ask how Mother was doing and about whether our projects went well. Even though we spent the afternoon together, his call lasted over an hour! As he was getting ready to hang up, he surprised me with another invitation. "I need to deliver papers over toward Neosho tomorrow. I don't have to be in the office because of the holiday. You are welcome to ride along with me if you want. We can have a little lunch on the way."

Of course, I was ready for a road trip anytime. We delivered his papers early and chattered like old friends as we gobbled down a hamburger and fries.

"I've always liked this part of Missouri," he said. "When I was in the Army, I spent time here at Camp Crowder. A bunch of us hungry service men often ate at a cafe in Neosho. I think it was called Bob Miller's. Whatever the name, I do remember their food was exceptional; especially their excellent bakery products."

After I told him I went through all twelve grades of school ten miles south of Neosho at Goodman, he wanted to see the school and where my family lived. "My mother probably made the bakery products you enjoyed at Bob Miller's. She was the baker there for years." I failed to tell him I was in the first or second grade when he was a soldier at Camp Crowder. Some things are better left unsaid.

Okay, so I guess I'm a slow learner. This preacher still acted more like an old comfy cousin or classmate than a boyfriend even though Wednesday was the fourth day in a row to see him. His visits were extremely casual and relaxed; more like old friends reconnecting than a date. Well, except he was so very kind, and there was that look!

Pastor Adams changing the church sign

13 - A THANKSGIVING DAY SURPRISE

"My cup overflows with blessings." Psalms 23:5 (NKJV)

November 1978

Early Thanksgiving morning I was surprised to get another call from that preacher. "Susie, one of the ladies from church will be at my house today fixing the turkey for our Single's Dinner. Do you have time to take a little drive with me and have lunch? I can pick you up in about an hour."

Well, there were two things I learned about Pastor Adams early on. He believed and lived the Bible cover-to-cover, and he knew what he wanted and did not hesitate to go after it.

The 'little' drive for lunch was to West Tulsa, Oklahoma, about a two-hour drive from Joplin. This time we were touring his hometown.

As we drove through the outskirts of the big city, he proudly pointed out where he grew up. He quickly admitted he was spoiled as a child. Being the youngest of eleven, most of the tough chores fell to the older children.

He talked freely of his childhood. By the time he was in school, many of his siblings had married and left home. I began to sense a love and a longing for his mother. He never said it in so many words, but I think he regretted leaving home early and not being there to take care of her when she grew older. She was a strong woman, loved and cared for her husband and children, and prayed faithfully for them every night.

His dad raised vegetables to sell at the farmer's market. He talked with pride and joy about loading a big truck on Saturday with their home-grown vegetables and taking them to town. This was hard work, but a momentous treat for him because, even as a young child, he liked meeting people. As a bonus, if sales were good, there was the promise of ice cream on the way home.

I recall being so engrossed in hearing his life story, I didn't even care what we ate for lunch. My spirit was soaking in every word like a sponge, I wanted to know more about what made this preacher man so different.

Apparently, he also did not want the day to end as he stopped at nearly every roadside park on the way back home to stretch our legs and sit on a picnic bench to talk.

"See you and your mother tonight," he said as he dropped me off at the house. "My sister, Nellie, is looking forward to meeting you both."

Later, I chuckled as Mother and I pulled up to the parsonage. It never dawned on me we both lived on Minnesota Street. His home was a beautiful brick parsonage with a fireplace and enclosed garage on a corner lot. I literally lived on the "other side of the tracks" in a tiny one-bedroom house on a small lot. Harmony Heights Baptist Church was on Indiana Street about midway between our two homes.

The aroma of turkey and trimmings permeated the air as we entered the front door. Inside, the tables were laden with tantalizing casseroles and desserts. Mother and I were made to feel welcome right away and enjoyed meeting new people we had not yet seen in church.

Other than the delicious meal, I honestly can't tell you much about the evening, whether there was a program or activity or not. Mother found a seat at the table next to Russell's sister, Nellie, and the conversation between the two was non-stop all evening. Turns out they had much in common, including having the same birth date.

As the evening wore on, I realized we were practically the only ones left. "Mother, we are about the last ones here. We need to head home."

The pastor walked us to the door and thanked us again for coming. Surprising myself as we were leaving, I commented softly, "I stay up until after midnight in case you want to call later." My mother gave me one of those looks—you know what that's like.

We had spent time together every day since Sunday. I felt like I finally had a friend I could confide in; one who really cared about me and what I thought. He definitely was not like any preacher I'd met before.

14 - FRIENDSHIP TAKES A TURN

"But as it is written, Eye hath not seen, nor ear heard, neither have entered into the heart of man, the things which God hath prepared for them that love him." 1 Corinthians 2:9 (KJV)

The next morning Mother was totally caught off guard when I called to let her know I was on my way over to spend Friday with her.

"Really? All day? That's great. Yes, I'll have coffee ready. We have all day together? Are you sure?"

The Singles' Department was a timely fit for Mother. She made new friends quickly and really delved into their good Bible studies. When I dared to ask her opinion of the pastor, she always gave the same short response: "He's nice. He's very nice."

I thought so, too. Nice, very nice.

Our Friday turned out to be the best of days. The air never felt fresher; the leaves were beginning to show their beautiful fall colors. Mother was well prepared to direct our entire day. After coffee at her house, we headed to her favorite restaurant for a good breakfast. This was followed by a few craft shows, a drive in the country to see the foliage, a little snack, and more shopping. She even found a tole painting class for us to attend. Yes, it was a fine outing.

Mother was going to be busy on Saturday with laundry and housecleaning and I had housework to catch up on as well. However, my phone was ringing off the hook early the next morning. "Susie, this is Russell. My sister, Nellie, took the kids home with her for the weekend. Are you free tonight? I made reservations for us at Beefmasters for seven o'clock. I can pick you up at six-thirty."

Reservations? Pick me up? Beefmasters - formal dining, expensive. Everything in me wanted to tell him our regular Wendy's or Bonanza was perfectly fine. I did not want to go to a fancy restaurant. But, when I opened my mouth, I told him it sounded great.

I lied. It didn't sound great to me. My fine dining experiences were few and not memorable in a positive way. I mean, how many forks does one need? All the extra dishes and silverware seemed a needless waste to me. After all, in my other life, I did my share of kitchen duty in those high-class places. And there was the thought of what I would wear to a fine restaurant. He will surely be wearing his very best. Oh, Lord, what am I getting into? I really need Your help.

There was a particular ambiance about the place: I did indeed feel special as we were led to a cozy corner table. Russell was calm and collected with a "no big deal attitude;" Susie was in a tizzy.

Obviously, neither of us were up on fine dining as we spent more time talking than eating our salad. We finally realized they were waiting for us to finish our salads before they brought the main course. Whether at home or in a restaurant, we talked non-stop. So much to say. So much to learn about one another and our families.

It was very late when we pulled up in front of my house. He was quick to open the car door for me, then slowly walked me to the door. Before I could say a word, he wrapped his strong arms around me and gave me a kiss. Wow! This most definitely was no friendship kiss! We stood and snuggled together in the cool night air for quite a while. He gave me a soft kiss on the cheek and big smile as he headed for his car. This had been a date, a real date. Thankfully, it was our one and only formal date, but definitely not the last of that preacher.

15 - PREACHER MAN HAD A PLAN

"Trust in the Lord with all your heart, And lean not on your own understanding." Proverbs 3:5 (KJV)

Before I could put my weary body to bed, the phone was ringing. Earlier, Russell failed to mention he made plans for our Sunday together. "After church in the morning, you can go with me to Nellie's. She and the kids are anxious to get to know you better. I will pick you up at your house after church. Don't eat because Nellie will have fried chicken, potatoes, gravy, and all the trimmings." He said he was praying for me and hung up the phone. No discussion.

There was a difference in the manner in which he made plans without asking me. In a few short days, he gained my respect and trust in such a way that I knew he desired the best for me and for his family. Not only did I know it was okay to agree, but I also knew I could decline with no argument.

Mildred Howerton and Mom working in the church nursery

Sunday morning, I was both relieved and surprised when Mother had plans to have lunch with the Singles' Class. Her desire to be with other ladies her age gave me real peace as my life seemed to be drastically changing overnight. Not only had Mother made friends, she had found a place to serve in the nursery.

The Rebel and Preacher Man

From the time Russell picked me up after church on Sunday until we got to Oklahoma, he talked almost non-stop about his kids. He was very proud of Michael, and Laura and of Debbie and her family, and was eager for me to get better acquainted with them.

Nellie lived in a small trailer in Vinita, Oklahoma. She was much like her little brother; her conversations were non-stop. We chatted over a table laden with fried chicken like Momma made, and enough extras for a hungry army.

I personally enjoyed watching the kids play. Early in our relationship, I wondered why God should allow me to be the mom to such remarkable children. I loved them from the first day I met them. I can't say I recall much of our trip home except it was non-stop chatter.

This was a turning point for us as Russell began bringing the kids to my house after school to study and often for supper. God had provided the perfect home for me alone; and for my new family to visit. A nice wall opening between the kitchen and living room provided a bit of privacy without totally separating us from the kids. From the couch in the living room, Russell and I could communicate with Mike and Laura as they did homework or crafts at the kitchen table.

Every day following our "big date," we were together, either with his family or mine. Of course, we continued to keep a neutral distance at church.

If you are reading this waiting for a romantic interlude when Preacher Man pops "the question," I will skip to the chase. This is it, seriously. About two weeks after Thanksgiving, Russell called to ask me if he could come by the house. He was on his way to a meeting in the association and only had a few minutes.

A man on mission, he gave me a hearty hug and gentle kiss on the cheek. Then, with no forewarning, he simply said: "I am sure God has brought us together."

I agreed. I knew our meeting was definitely God ordained.

He continued, "I love you and I believe you love me, too. I know Michael and Laura love you as well. I think we should get married, don't you?"

"Yes, I do." We hugged, kissed and snuggled a bit (well-- quite a bit)! Then he went out to win the world while I loaded my tools, wallpaper, and paint to finish a job I had been putting off. I can say I wasn't putting it off any longer. I was on "Cloud 9", and my feet were barely touching the ground as I readied myself to head to Carthage. I can attest to the fact that, as you walk closer and closer to the Lord, He makes every step you take more positively certain. I cannot explain the peace and joy, I felt because of the assurance of God's direction in my life concerning this preacher.

The next Sunday I could hardly wait for the morning worship service. I knew I was finally home in more ways than I could count. Mother was a bit surprised when I rushed up during the invitation. I joined the church on promise of a letter from the First Baptist Church in Goodman, Missouri.

To keep talk in the church and community to the minimum, we decided not to tell anyone including our families about our engagement until right before he presented me to the church. I'm sure Mother and my brother as well as his family knew we had more than a casual friendship.

16 - INTRODUCING ME TO THE CHURCH

"And the Lord God said, It is not good that the man should be alone; I will make him an help meet for him." Genesis 2:18 (KJV)

December 10, 1978

Autumn in the Ozarks sports a crispness in the air unlike any other season. Sturdy oaks and maples flaunt their colors and begin to shed for a winter's rest. My coast-to-coast travels never found anything to compare. It's a romantic time; a time for family, for snuggling by the fire, for sharing good news. And so, it was on a cool Sunday morning, Mother and I took our places with the Singles' Class in the crowded sanctuary for worship.

My hungry soul rejoiced within me as Director Bill Sutter led the choir and congregation. How I loved Jesus. How I wanted to worship Him more every day. How thankful I was for what God was doing in my life. Mother, too, was rejoicing. Not only did she have her daughter in church with her, but also a host of new friends to fill her empty days.

As Pastor Adams began his message, he asked the congregation to turn in their Bibles to the second chapter of Genesis, verses seven and eight, as he boldly told the story of God's creation of mankind.

"And the LORD God formed man of the dust of the ground, and breathed into his nostrils the breath of life; and man became a living soul."

Continuing his message in verse eighteen and following, I wondered if the congregation suspected a motive behind his preaching about marriage.

"And the LORD God said, It is not good that the man should be alone; I will make him an help meet for him. And out of the ground the LORD God formed every beast of the field, and every fowl of the air; and brought them unto Adam to see what he would call them: and whatsoever Adam called every living creature, that was the name thereof. And Adam gave names to all cattle, and to the fowl of the air, and to every beast of the field; but for Adam there was not found an help meet for him. And the LORD God caused a deep sleep to fall upon Adam, and he slept: and he took one of his ribs, and closed up the flesh instead thereof; And the rib, which the LORD God had taken from man, made he a woman, and brought her unto the man. And Adam said, This is now bone of my bones, and flesh of my flesh: she shall be called Woman, because she was taken out of Man. Therefore shall a man leave his father and his mother, and shall cleave unto his wife: and they shall be one flesh."

Genesis 2:18-24

He closed his message with the normal invitation hymn and call to the altar. When those who came forward finished praying and returned to their seats, Pastor Adams asked the congregation to please be seated.

"I want to thank you for your love and support for me and my family. You are a wonderful, loving church. I am thankful to be your pastor. *"*

"Beloved," he continued. "We prayed, and the Lord sent me a wife." With that being said, he asked me to come forward. "I am happy to tell you God answered our prayers and has sent Susie here to be my wife and a mother to my children. I am sure you will grow to love her as my family and I have."

There was a distinct stillness, looks of surprise, then a few hearty claps as the congregation tried to comprehend what their pastor was saying.

Consider the facts. In January of that year, Harmony Heights Baptist church had an old-fashioned food pounding to fill their new pastor's pantry. In addition, they brought silver dollars to make a chain for Russell and Marcella's twenty-fifth wedding anniversary. They supported him and helped provide for his little children during the next few months as his wife's health deteriorated.

I joined the church November 26, another member of the ever-changing Single Adult Department. He had not been widowed long; he was in his fifties and his bride-to-be in her thirties.

As God would have it, the date he made our engagement public was December 10, my thirty-sixth birthday! Wow! What an amazing birthday present! Thank you, Jesus!

17 - AS IF IT HAPPENED: THE REBEL UNDER PRESSURE

"Be confident, my heart, because the Lord has been good to me."
Psalms 116:7 (GNT)

When a Southern Baptist church extends a call to a minister to become their pastor, he will go through background checks and interviews - many pretty rigid. Their wives are often interviewed to some extent as well.

Of course, it wouldn't apply here since Russell was already their pastor. However, let's suppose a committee decided I should be interviewed since they didn't know me. It could have gone much like this:

"Well, Susie, we are so glad you are here. We have been extremely pleased with Brother Adams' pastorate for the past two years. As he is now considering marriage, we have a few questions for you. We are sure you know as a pastor's wife; you will automatically be in the limelight. And, as time goes on, you will be assuming leadership responsibilities as well. Tell us, what is your full name?"

"My full name is Carrol Sue Kinslow Mabry."

"So, you have been married before?"

"Yes, my husband, Bob, died of a heart attack at age of forty-four."

"I see. Do you have any children?"

"Yes, I have a son, Rick Hall."

Feet shuffled and backs stiffened as one committee member voiced their concern over his last name. "Oh, you had another marriage? Have you been divorced?"

"No. We did not change Rick's last name when he came to live with us at age ten."

There was an obvious sigh of relief. "Good. Tell us about your education."

"Sure. I attended all twelve years of school in Goodman, Missouri. I graduated in 1960."

There was a long pause, obviously they were waiting for more. "Go ahead, tell us about your college; where did you go and what were your majors?"

The rebel was beginning to rise within me. I replied with a firm voice, "That's it. Everything I know I got from the 'School of Hard Knocks!'" Big smile... mine, not theirs.

By now the committee was not sure what to do with me. "Let's move on. Tell us about your salvation and your church experience."

Finally, they were getting around to something important. "My parents did not attend church, but my brother and I were faithful. I gave my heart to Jesus at age thirteen and He has never left. All through high school I was involved in church activities, Bible schools, camps, and any opportunity to learn more about the Bible."

"I can see you were very faithful as a child. We want to hear about your church experiences after you left school."

"I don't have any more to tell."

A committee of seven adults sat petrified, unable to comprehend what they heard. Was their pastor going to marry a woman who didn't even go to church? "You what? You never attended church after you left high school? Can we ask you, what do you intend to do in the church after you marry our pastor?"

"Nothing!" There was a calmness in my spirit which had to

come from God. The blank stares let me know I gave an inadequate reply.

I straightened myself up in the chair, tidied my skirt, and smiled. "When we are married, I intend to support my husband in all he does. I will pray with and for him every day. I will take care of our family and stand ready to serve Jesus whenever and wherever needed."

Completely at a loss for words, the committee struggled to know where to go next. Finally, the chairman voiced one more question. "Obviously, you do not personally have the education or experience to assume the role of a pastor's wife in our church. What qualifies you?"

At this point it was a good thing they could not read my mind. With a broad smile I said: "Well, I love your pastor."

"That's all well and good, Susie, but we have a class full of single ladies that 'love our pastor'. What else can you tell us?"

Confident of the Holy Spirit at work in my heart, I replied in a polite but firm voice: "Jesus Christ is my First Love. I know He drew us together. His Holy Spirit will equip me for the tasks He has for me when He is ready. In the meantime, I will continue my daily routine of personal Bible study and prayer. I will readily serve when and where He leads."

The atmosphere in the room changed slightly. Although the committee was still a bit apprehensive, they replied. "Welcome to our church, Susie. Truly God has sent you our way."

***

While this interview never actually happened, it is important for you to know every one of the facts I stated here are true. With no formal education or training or church experience, and a background that would shock most faithful church members, I

The Rebel and Preacher Man

was the least likely person to be put in any position of leadership or influence.

However, God had plans for my life from the day I was born. During my forty-two years of marriage to Preacher Man, God used the life experiences He allowed me to go through to give me the courage and ability to serve in the roles He had for me. I genuinely and humbly praise Him every day of my life, for His Grace, and Love for a stubborn, country rebel.

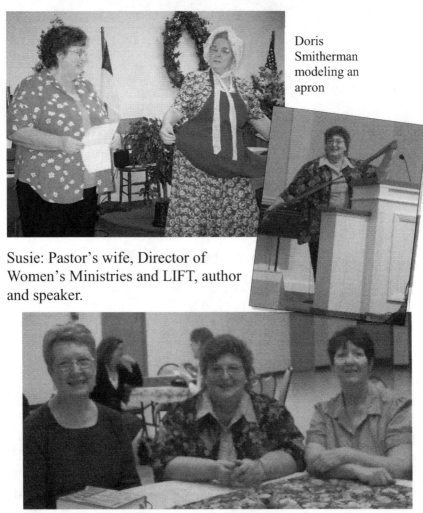

Doris Smitherman modeling an apron

Susie: Pastor's wife, Director of Women's Ministries and LIFT, author and speaker.

Regina, Susie, Pam at a St. Clair, MO Retreat

18 - BRIDE AND GROOM COUNSELING

"Seek the Lord and His strength, seek His face continually."
I Chronicles 16:11 (KJV)

While the interview at church never happened, I was not off the hook. I was about to get a first-hand look at what being a pastor's wife was like as we began to prepare for our wedding.

"Do you have anyone you want to perform our wedding ceremony?" Russell posed the question to me without hesitation. He truly had no clue I not only did not know someone, but I also had little desire to spend time with preachers. (It's a good thing God doesn't reveal his entire plans all at once!)

"No, honey. I'm okay with anyone you choose. Do you have anyone you want to ask?"

Of course, he did. A good friend of his, Pastor Glen Pence, of the First Baptist Church, Joplin, was his first choice. Russell said we could give him a tentative date and then work it out later with the family.

> **Interesting fact:** Glen Pence pastored in Buffalo in the late sixties and early seventies. He preached the Dallas County Association's annual sermon in 1967 and 1971. God eventually led Russell to a ministry as Director of Missions in Buffalo in 2000.

The first order of business was to meet the preacher in his office for a brief get acquainted time. I figured he would simply get our legal names, what kind of ceremony we wanted, and the date and time for the rehearsal. Wrong! Russell's beloved Dr. Pence scheduled three counseling sessions. Seriously, THREE? What am I getting myself into?

Later Russell told me Brother Glen questioned him about how long we had known each other, did he know any of my background, etc. When Russell assured him that he and Harmony

Heights Baptist Church had been in prayer for a long time for God to provide a wife for him and a mother for his children, Bro. Pence was satisfied.

On the other hand, there was me. I'm not sure he knew quite what to think of this happy-go-lucky, crazy young gal that had her eyes on the preacher. All of Joplin was aware of how the Single Adult Department at Harmony Heights grew quickly once their handsome pastor became widowed.

His first session with me was to get acquainted. He wanted to make sure I was a Christian, I believed the Bible cover to cover, and I believed marriage was a life-time commitment. He also wanted to hear my opinion of having a ready-made family.

The second meeting with Rev. Pence caught me off guard. With a sincere, almost cold expression, his first question was overwhelming. "Young lady, do you have any idea what you are getting into?" (NOTE: On hindsight I can say, I had no clue, but I would do it over again in a heartbeat.)

He went on to explain all "Christians" in a church do not necessarily display Christ in their actions, especially toward the pastor. Obviously, he spoke from personal experience when he continued. "There will be times when those you regard highly will turn on their pastor, your husband. A few will do all they can to encourage him and his family to leave. Because of Christ in your heart, you will have to love them anyway. You will have to protect your personal relationship with Jesus as you continue to serve in a difficult place."

He continued for several minutes. "Russell is a well-loved pastor and, I think a good preacher. As his wife, you may want to question his messages from time-to-time. You will need to walk closely to the Lord and trust Him to make any changes He needs in your husband. It is not your job to plan His sermons!" That made me wonder at this point if we met somewhere in the past; he seemed to know me all too well.

Rev. Pence left no stone unturned as he talked about my responsibilities as a mother and homemaker. By the time we finished the second session, I felt like I was applying for a job and most likely failed the test.

The entire mood changed in the third and final counseling session as Russell and I met together in his office. "Russell and Susie, I can see the Lord has surely put the two of you together. The love you have for one another is obviously a gift from God. I am happy for you, for young Michael and Laura, and for your older children and your grandchildren."

We were secure in our love and in the call of God upon our lives. The only thing holding us back from becoming a family now was the wedding.

19 - ABOUT OUR CHILDREN

"But Jesus called them to Him and said, "Let the little children come to Me, and do not forbid them; for of such is the kingdom of God." Luke 18:16 (KJV)

When the two became one, there were adjustments to be made, not only by us but our children. A major challenge in writing this story of a preacher, his new wife and their various ministries is in giving ample time to talk about the four amazing children we were blessed to call ours.

Our four children could easily pen their own books, zoning in on their lives as they adjusted to different lifestyles and parenting skills while trying to make their own mark. The one qualifying factor: every child knew they were loved but there were major adjustments for each one.

RICKY

On a rainy Saturday, ten-year-old Ricky left his home in Williamsburg, Virginia with his parents and sister to visit friends and relatives across the state in Roanoke. With no or little "heads up," he left Virginia with a man he did not remember and woman he had never met. In addition to having a new mom and dad overnight, he gained an uncle, Richard. Through the years many assumed Ricky was named after his Uncle Richard. My parents became Ricky's first grandparents, a role which they played quite well. Then, as a young father, his new dad, Bob, suddenly passed away. Ricky was married with two children of his own when Russell and I married.

DEBBIE

Russell and Marcella raised Debbie from age ten. Debbie and Tom were married on Marcella's birthday with young Michael and Laura by her side.

About the time Russell and Marcella's family moved from Clinton, Missouri to Joplin, Marcella was diagnosed with terminal cancer and given only a few months to live. She lived sixteen months. I am convinced God allowed her more time for many reasons, not the least of which was the country-wide prayer support for a pastor left with two small children to raise.

Consider this: On September 4th, 1978, Daughter Debbie and Tom celebrated their wedding anniversary, and Debbie gave birth to their first child. September fourth was also Marcella's birthday. As I think of it now, I wonder if Debbie had anyone to talk with about her mother not being there to celebrate with them.

LAURA

Back at the parsonage was a busy pastor with two little ones who needed personal attention. Laura lost the only mother she had ever known. Two months later, her older sister had a baby, and she became Aunt Laura. Another two months and her dad was dating a new lady. Two months more – a wedding! A lot to take in for a young girl.

MICHAEL

Michael was four when he was adopted; so, he knew a little about his birth family. Nonetheless, losing this mother had to be very hard on an eleven-year-old boy.

Before either of our families had sufficient time to grieve the loss of a spouse and parent, the scene changed drastically; Russell

The Rebel and Preacher Man

and I met, wed, and combined families. As I look back on those days, I will have to say our children seemed to adapt quickly to their new mom. I didn't know anything about their daily routines, their food preferences, or personal lifestyles. All I knew for sure was God put us together and I loved each of them with a depth which surely came from God.

I am extremely thankful Michael and Laura were not uprooted from their home at age ten like Ricky and Debbie. The younger ones were safe and secure in a familiar place. Routines for them remained the same so far as school, church, and other activities.

Getting married in a record-breaking blizzard meant our newly formed family unit could get acquainted while travel and activities were limited. Truly the Hand of God was at work January 13, 1979.

20 - MOTHER'S TRADITIONAL CHRISTMAS BREAKFAST

"O, Give thanks to the Lord! Call upon His name; make known His deeds among the people." 1 Chronicles 16:8 (KJV)

Two weeks after Russell announced our engagement to the church and amid making wedding plans, Mother wanted to have her traditional Christmas breakfast for our family. I questioned whether she should do it with so much going on. We did have a wedding to plan and church activities to attend. I reminded her there was more than one or two additional people to feed.

"Carrol Sue, how could you even think we could skip our Christmas breakfast? Why should this year be any different. I am surprised at you even thinking that!" Yep, Carrol Sue was in trouble with Momma again!

She continued. "I am happy for you and what God is doing in your life. I love your new family and I want every single one of them to feel welcome in my home any time. You haven't given our family much time to get to know Russell and the children. Our breakfast will provide a good opportunity for that to happen. I expect you to make sure everyone in his family is encouraged to come."

This promised to be quite the day as family poured into Momma's little house from far and wide. Mother's sister, Josie, and her friend came early to help in the kitchen. Her kids, Penny and Earl, brought a few friends. My brother, Richard, and my son Ricky and their families rounded out the Kinslow clan.

Enter Pastor Adams and his two children, his married daughter, Debbie, and her family. My family had not been around

The Rebel and Preacher Man

many church folk, let alone a preacher. Each one quickly proclaimed to be Christians though they did not attend church at the present time. I will leave the conversation there for you to ponder.

I do not know where Mother found all the tables and chairs we needed for breakfast. We were seated in a line from the kitchen, through the dining room and into the living room. Neither do I know how she prepared and stored all that bounty in her tiny kitchen.

The beautifully adorned tables were laden with sausage, ham and bacon, biscuits and gravy, potatoes, and eggs. There were pancakes and an assortment of home-made jellies, syrups, and honey. Coffee, juices, milk, and even a pitcher of water for the thirsty. She even prepared a variety of hot and cold cereals; and had fresh fruits available. Of course, my mother was a professional cook and baker; no restaurant in town could hold a candle to her festive buffet.

The breakfast and the entire day were perfect in every way. Most were meeting my husband-to-be and his family for the first time. Russell had a way of making people feel comfortable, often adding a bit of levity to the conversations. During the day, he and my brother had a couple of very serious conversations I would like to have heard. However, they were kept private. It became apparent through the years my brother gained a deep respect for Russell and often confided in him, for which I am thankful. It was, after all, my brother who would give me away on my wedding day.

A warm unbidden tear runs down my cheek as I close my eyes to smell those biscuits one more time. I can almost hear the laughter of a family only God could draw together. Forever etched in my memory is my brother's broadening smile as he wrapped his strong arms around me and said, "Sis, you done real good this time!"

In honor of my Little Brother - Richard Frank Kinslow 10-27-44 — 11-8-17

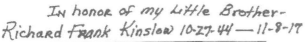

Mother's 1978 Christmas Breakfast

Richard 'n' Connie & son Andy

A Mother's Delight — Working with Richard on sisters' wedding

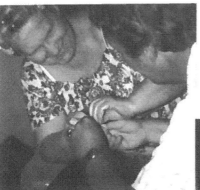

Brother knew every critter and plant on Adams' Acres —

21 - A CHRISTMAS LIKE NO OTHER

"There is a time for everything, and a season for every activity under the heavens; …a time to mourn and a time to dance…" Ecclesiastes 3:1,4 (KJV)

CHRISTMAS 1978

How do I tell about Christmas 1978 and give it the justice it deserves? I still can barely comprehend it all myself, and it has been a few years. This I know - one day I was alone, so very alone. Sure, there was family nearby – a loving son, Ricky, and his family and my extremely patient, loving mother. But my little house on Minnesota Street now quite often felt very empty and too quiet.

There was not a doubt in my mind, My Loving Heavenly Father sent Preacher Man and his two little munchkins into my life. Already I knew this was more than I ever dared dream of.

This was my first Christmas alone and, up until a few weeks before, I didn't seem to have much to celebrate. (The "Reason for the Season" aside.) A small green tree with red bows on it stood alone on a corner table with a few small gifts under it.

Things changed overnight when Russell announced to the church that we were to become a family. He began to bring Mike and Laura to my house more often to do their homework and have supper. I loved those two so much; at times I questioned God allowing me to be their mother. When Russell attended late meetings, I went to the parsonage so the kids could get to bed on time. Well at least there was the opportunity to go to bed on time.

My favorite memory as we were getting acquainted was being in the parsonage with them making decorations and trimming their Christmas tree. Each child told stories of Christmas, a favorite gift, or something on their personal wish lists. Laura was learning to play the piano and often tickled those ivories as I sat in wonder at what God had wrought in my life. It

-1978-
Fun way to get to know Michael & Laura

was a time of bonding with two golden treasures God graciously entrusted to my care.

The parsonage was in the middle of a section of homes that put luminaries out a few days before Christmas. The kids were eager to teach me what luminaries were and how to prepare them for the season. First a bit of sand was put in the bottom of enough paper bags to line the sidewalk, driveway, and the edge of the yard. In each bag a tea lite candle was then secured in the sand. The candles had to be kept lit from dusk into the night as streams of cars drove by to see the wonder of it all. Energetic young Michael was readily available, lighter in hand, should any candles burn out.

Our first December at Harmony Heights Baptist was also a time of refreshing for Mother and me. We quickly joined in on all their Christmas activities as we embraced our new church family. From a beautiful Cantata on Sunday morning to an elaborate Tasting Tea at night, Mother and I were welcomed and felt right at home as we celebrated Jesus's birth. Add traditional Christmas caroling to nursing homes and communities; no leaf was left unturned.

This was only a preview of the marvelous things God had in store for two widows who four months earlier felt compelled to search for a church home.

22 - OUR WEDDING IS WHEN?

"But my God shall supply all your need according to his riches in glory by Christ Jesus." Philippians 4:19 (KJV)

Somehow, in the midst of our busy schedules, we needed to focus on planning our wedding. While doing crafts at my house, the kids and I made a big calendar to mark off the days until we became a family. We were ready now; however, Preacher Man knew the church needed time to process all the changes. There had been several major adjustments in the pastor's life since he was called there less than two years earlier.

My life at this point is proof positive that God looks after His children and cares for their every need. Practically overnight, my entire lifestyle changed drastically. I had not been involved in any fellowships or group activities other than work-related since graduating from high school. After Bob died, I worked alone. My only outside activities were with family, most often Mother.

I absolutely had no clue what to bring to a "carry-in dinner" or church-wide fellowship. When I asked Russell what kind of snacks to bring to a Single Adult gathering, he said, "You know, something like those little yellow puffy things. Anything will do." ??? Obviously he liked snacks like cheese puffs, chips, and sweets.

Almost overnight, everyone knew who I was and I knew few more than my family-to-be. They immediately made Mother and me welcome and they helped us feel comfortable no matter what we were doing.

Of course, November and December are not the most convenient times to plan a wedding on short notice. In the works already at Harmony Heights was an elaborate Christmas Cantata and annual Tasting Tea. Various children's programs were in full swing. An elaborate New Year's Eve program began at six o'clock with dinner followed by four hours of family activities, snacks, music, and projects. At eleven, everyone met in the sanctuary to close out the year with music, preaching, and an altar of prayer at midnight.

February seemed out of the question with Valentine activities the second week. We finally settled on January 27. In a short time, we moved the date to the 20th and finally the 13th.

JANUARY 13? That was less than one month to prepare for a church wedding! We had to check Rev. Pence's calendar so invitations could be sent right away. There was choosing the wedding party and the attire for them and for us. Add to those, flowers, and food, and...! Only God!

It wasn't simply lack of time that could have been a stumbling block. The bride-to-be (me) never attended a formal wedding in her life, and frankly had no desire to do so. The few weddings I remembered, including my own, took place in a pastor's home or church with few attendees and no extras.

Mother was elated. She could finally help her daughter prepare for her wedding. Time and shopping venues were limited; we needed to find the bride's dress first and choose colors to compliment her dress.

When no suitable bride's dress could be found in all of Joplin, we headed to the one small dress shop in nearby Carthage. By God's grace, the perfect dress was found. A light green princess-style dress with long sleeves and a V-shaped neckline "just happened" to be my size. For my beautiful Mother, a flowing long dress in muted grays and soft pinks which made her red hair dazzle.

Having found the dresses, we chose light green and soft pink for the colors. The church rallied and found seamstresses eager to make the attendant's dresses using a pink double-knit fabric. A tailor made Michael a tan double-knit suit. I'm sure it wasn't what an eleven-year-old boy would have chosen, but he remained silent. Of course, his new mom and his grandmother thought he was quite handsome.

With help from more experienced women in the church, we got invitations, napkins, and other details taken care of in plenty of time. These gals brought up needs I was not aware of like rehearsal dinner, thank you gifts, guest book attendant, etc.

Within a few days, our checklist was complete. That is everything except one not-so-small detail. I was a bit uncertain. Was it proper to have feather flowers in the big, fancy sanctuary? What would the church or our families think?

The rebel in me quietly decided it WAS my wedding after all; I should do whatever I wanted!

23 - FEATHER FLOWERS AND LITTLE BROTHER'S ANXIETY

"Therefore my heart is glad, and my glory rejoices; My flesh also will rest in hope." Psalm 16:9 (KJV)

January 1979

"Mother, does the church actually know about all my sister's plans for their preacher's wedding?" Richard stared at Mother's dining table overflowing with pink, green, and white turkey feathers. "I don't think they are going to like this stuff in their fancy church."

"Son, Russell has seen Susie's flowers before. He told her to do whatever she wanted. This is not something you should worry about."

Little brother's reply was quick and to the point. "Mother! Seriously? If that preacher starts off by letting my sister do what she wants, you better pray for the church!"

My engagement to a preacher took my entire family by surprise. Richard was quick to give me one of those 'if-that's-what-you-really- want-to-do' looks. Nevertheless, he previously voiced his approval, although he had little if anything in common with Russell or the church.

Both Mom and Brother questioned the difference in our ages fearing I might be taking care of 'that old man' someday. I overheard my mother tell my brother to relax. "Perhaps your sister will finally settle down and quit traipsing all over the country."

By spending time creating our own flowers, God in His wisdom provided a natural opportunity for our families to get acquainted. Russell and Richard spent hours chatting as they watched us turn piles of colorful feathers into beautiful flowers.

Both were surprised at their common interests. Neither

lacked communication skills. The flower project became a fun, family time.

My earliest childhood memories are of Mother and me working on creative projects together. It may have been cooking, sewing, sketching and, or painting. With no extra monies, Mother had a knack for creating beautiful items from whatever she had on hand. I missed my mother terribly through the years and welcomed this opportunity to be with her; it was the best of times.

Working together, it wasn't long until piles of feathers turned into tall pink gladiolas and fluffy white mums. The stems were adorned with lime green turkey feather leaves. Curled dark green goose feathers made the gladiolas a work of art. We created lavish garlands of curled white, pink, and green feathers to line the stage area. Flat centerpieces of white mums, pink rosebuds, ostrich plumes and colorful ribbons adorned the tables and every flat surface in the entry and reception hall. Tiny white goose feathers were perfect for pretty bells to hang over the serving table.

For the wedding bouquet, boutonnieres and corsages, Cousin Penny and Aunt Josie came to the rescue with beautiful creations of silk flowers and greenery. Our mid-winter wedding showed the promise of springtime with those beautiful colors. Time was short; we spent many long days and nights creating our extravagant masterpieces.

Surely there was stress as we rushed to meet our impossible deadline. If so, it missed me completely. Spending those days in Mom's warm home with plenty of coffee, food, and those I loved cannot be explained.

The relationships built between our families in a few short weeks were molded to last through a lifetime of change and challenge.

24 - OUR WEDDING

"Therefore a man shall leave his father and his mother and hold fast to his wife, and the two shall become one flesh."
Genesis 2:24 (KJV)

JANUARY 13, 1979

Light snowflakes sparkled in the moonlight as I snuggled into bed at Momma's for the last time. Tomorrow my life would be forever changed as Little Brother and Mother would give me to Preacher Man. Nothing could prepare me for what God planned for me and my family as I yielded my life to His control.

By morning, the "light snow" turned into blizzard conditions. Russell called to make sure we could safely get to the church in Joplin from Webb City. He was telling callers, "If the preacher makes it, the wedding is on!" Although the soloist and dozens of guests were forced to stay home, there were sixty plus including my relatives from forty miles away. After all, having a preacher as part of our family was quite the event!

Being a bit preoccupied for the moment, I missed capturing the picture of the year: the arrival of our wedding cake. Not the cake so much, as it was the drama of getting it out of the delivery van and into the church. White van, white cake, white blinding snow literally pouring from the sky as the delivery team clad in white coats wrangled the cake from the van into the church. Hilarious to watch, although a bit scary for them!

Tensions eased as the minister, Rev. Glen Pence, arrived early in his fancy suitcoat and tie, blue jeans, and boots! Another missed Kodak moment.

This elated bride thought her new family was quite the picture of perfection decked out in beautiful pink and brown attire. And the handsome groom in his trim, double-knit suit? Oh, my, be still my heart!

My dashing little brother, Richard, was all smiles as he walked me down the aisle. Today he was exceptionally positive - although I'm sure he still had more than a few doubts about his sister's latest venture.

Totally engulfed in the moment, I felt like Cinderella at the ball. How could my wild, carefree early years ever come to this point? Surely God over-extended His Grace to this rebellious country girl.

All too quickly came Brother Pence's words, "Russell and Susie Adams, I now pronounce you husband and wife. Russell, you may kiss your bride." And... kiss he did!

My first opportunity to share the tremendous love God poured into my heart and soul happened as we turned to walk down the aisle. We paused as I leaned over to kiss my beautiful mother. Seeing the peace, love, and contentment in her eyes as she took a rose from my hand, melted my heart. She smiled at

Two blessed ladies – My mother and me!

us and quickly gave my groom a wink of approval. Neither of us could be prepared for what God had in store for His girls as Preacher Man became one of the family.

The Rebel and Preacher Man

Miraculously, as the storm continued to rage outside, no one hurried to leave. As our family and friends spent time getting acquainted, many questioned where we were going on our honeymoon. We knew in our hearts the treacherous storm most likely prevented shenanigans from our families or from the church. We did indeed have definite honeymoon plans, but not even our family could imagine what they were.

For the record: According to the University of Missouri Climate Center, the state recorded an average winter temperature of 24.1 in the winter of 1978-1979. That was the worst recorded winter in the history of southern Missouri. Who knew? Storms or no storms, the Russell Adams family was ready to face the future together.

It was the best of times.

25 - PERFECT HONEYMOON DESTINATION

"Delight yourself in the Lord, and He shall give you the desires of your heart." Psalm 37:4 (KJV)

Even though we both had been married before, Russell and I took extra care to ensure a memorable honeymoon. We were convinced God drew us together in unbelievable times and circumstances. We were like teenagers again experiencing our first love.

Tom and Debbie seemed eager to take young Michael and Laura home with them while we were gone. This alleviated much of our concern as it also provided our kids with a small window of time to adjust to their rapidly changing environment.

We were definitely on the same page regarding where we wanted to spend our honeymoon; we wanted our first nights together to be in our own home – not in a motel.

Planning ahead, we parked my old Chevrolet truck in plain sight on the front lot of the Joplin Holiday Inn on busy Range Line Road. Getting wind of our wedding, the motel changed their marque to read: Congratulations Newlyweds, Pastor Russell and Susie Adams. Because of the blizzard conditions, our names were left on the marque for weeks.

A few days before our wedding, we stocked the refrigerator and freezer with everything we could possibly want for an entire week.

After the wedding, we headed for Bonanza to enjoy a steak supper with all the trimmings. We knew we were safe. It was still snowing profusely; no one was going to be spying on us to see where we went next. Our hearts and tummies were full to the brim, it was time to head home.

As Russell pulled the car into the garage, blinding snow quickly covered his tracks. We enjoyed several days of cuddling, eating the best of foods, and listening to our favorite gospel music as we sat by the fire. Not only was it romance at its best, but I also knew this man would never cause me harm or abandon me.

We were not too concerned as winter continued to rage outside. Michael and Laura were safe and well taken care of, as were our older two children and their families. We were thankful we chose to honeymoon in our home as there was no need to be out on the roads.

Hallmark Movies had nothing on us; our honeymoon was grand in every respect. As we talked about our backgrounds, friends, and families, the more we realized God truly put us together. Our individual plans and hopes for the future could not have been scripted any better.

Yet, as exciting as our days and nights were, I could sense something was beginning to bother Preacher Man. "Honey, you seem terribly quiet tonight. Where are your thoughts?"

His response was quick. "I miss the kids. I know they are okay with Tom and Debbie, but I miss them." Truthfully, we both wanted our kids to celebrate with us. By Monday we were calling Debbie to let her know we needed our kids with us to make our family complete.

Susie Kinslow Adams

26 - FREE TO BE ME

"Commit to the Lord whatever you do, and he will establish your plans."
Proverbs 16:3 (NIV)

Had Russell and I filled out one of those popular Compatibility Tests, either one of us may have earned a score of 20%-- maybe.

He spent his first thirty plus years without Jesus. I spent about the same amount of time running from Jesus. Age wise, I could easily have been his daughter.

After twenty-five years of marriage with its ups and downs, he struggled through sixteen months knowing his first love was going Home to be with Jesus. I was left alone after seventeen years of marriage with not even a few seconds' warning.

The list is endless of why we should not be married according to reasoning and common-sense evaluations. There was, however, one thing we knew for certain we had in common, only one, and His name is Jesus. Because of Jesus and His love for us, we allowed the Holy Spirit to work in and through our differences.

I did not understand or agree with all my illustrious husband did or said but I loved and accepted him as he was.

He was strong when he needed to be; he did not give in to my every whim. He was, in all respects, always the head of our household. For that, I am eternally grateful.

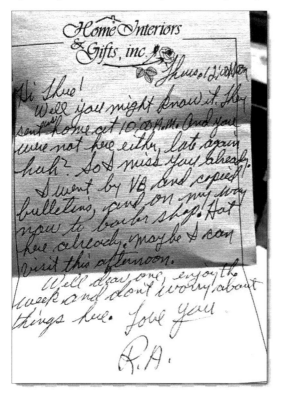

Right off the bat, Russell gave me the best gift anyone could give another: he let me be me. He had faith in me, yes, he did! Truth be told here; his greatest faith was in the One who created me. I'm sure he pleaded often for God's Holy Spirit to touch and soften my edges.

When he talked to me about our life in the parsonage, he let me know his doors were open, day or night, for those who may need him. And I was quick to let him know he needed to tell them I don't wear shoes, I don't clean house, and I'm not changing. But I do agree with him, anyone is welcome to come to our home any time.

Together, Russell and I attended every state and local convention, pastor and wife event, and missionary program that we could. He also encouraged me to sign up for any women's conferences or retreats in the area or in the convention. As I look back, I can see all these meetings served to educate me in the workings of the Missouri Baptist Convention.

He understood my deepest need to be by myself from time to time. "There will be times when I need a 'Susie Day'. I want to be able to head out of town for the day with no questions asked. I need personal, unscheduled space occasionally."

There are two things I feel extremely important to mention here. First, his letting me be me meant I earned his trust. He knew I would not do anything that violated our marriage or family values. Secondly, we bathed all our decisions, large and small in prayer and trusted Jesus to work out any differences we may have.

27 - MRS. PREACH IN TRAINING

*"Behold, I will do a new thing; now it shall spring forth; shall ye not know it?
I will even make a way in the wilderness, and rivers in the desert."*
Isaiah 43:19 (KJV)

Russell's children made me feel like family from day one. The next service after he announced our engagement, Mother and I took our regular places with the Single Adult Department. His older daughter, Debbie, was quick to approach me. "Mom, don't you think you should come sit over here with your family?" It is impossible to describe what those words meant to me.

While still skeptical, the congregation could see God's plan as the pastor's little children snuggled up next to me on Sunday. My heart could barely contain the love I had for the family God was entrusting to my care.

Russell never expected me to be more than I was. His love and respect for me in those early years gave me confidence to stretch and grow as God led. Even in the past years when I was not attending church, I believed God heard and answered my prayers. I felt His Holy Spirit tug at my heartstrings even in my rebellion.

Yes, I believed in prayer-private prayer between me and God. But public prayer was for pastors and church leaders, or so I thought. However, deacons Anson Cox and Lloyd Piquard and other church leaders called on me to pray at every opportunity. I will never forget feeling my face turn beet red and sweat popping out the first time I stood in a crowded dining hall asking God to bless the food. The prayer was quick and to the point.

I was convinced it was a church-wide conspiracy. "Remember," some said, "you are simply talking to God. He

The Rebel and Preacher Man

wants to hear from you." My rebellious spirit wanted to let them know God did not need me to pray out loud. I will forever be grateful for God's obedient children at Harmony Heights Baptist Church who lovingly helped their pastor's new wife grow in grace and knowledge.

Every Sunday night, the church met for Church Training (now called Discipleship Training). Short parts were assigned from the lesson in a quarterly study book to be presented the following week. Yes, of course, Susie was always given a part to prepare. Each week I bravely stood, wiping sweat from my brow as I spent maybe two minutes quickly reading my part. On-the-job training. Mercy, they were a patient congregation.

Not to worry, God had a crash course planned for me to practice praying and speaking in a group. In the first year of our marriage, the church secretary, Linda, and I started an exercise program at church. We chose the name LIFT Class - an acronym for Ladies Improving the Father's Temple.

Scripture and prayer were added since we were, after all, meeting at church. Within weeks, the scripture reading grew into a Bible Study as more ladies joined us. LIFT now stood for Ladies in Fellowship Together and exercise was left to the gym.

Another first for me was a church-wide Family Retreat Harmony Heights sponsored in 1982, It was scheduled from Friday night through supper on Saturday. Entire families headed to the campground to worship and play together. Qualified teams led each age group from preschool through senior adults, couples, and singles. Studies, recreation, worship times, and mealtimes were well organized. God provided this rebel heart a beautiful picture of what it means to be a part of a loving church family. The adults and children returned home on Saturday night. Sunday morning services were scheduled as usual. Worship was more meaningful to me as we heard how God worked in families and individuals over the weekend. The youth returned home in time to participate in the evening service. Overwhelming!

Joplin Senior High School was across the road from the church providing an abundant opportunity to reach kids. The church provided free breakfast and snacks early Friday mornings with guest speakers or musicians. This ministry provided a casual way for HHBC youth to invite their friends to church.

Both Russell and I took every Seminary Extension class offered in our area. As finals were given on every Old and New Testament Study, we eagerly compared our grades. God refreshed my memory and increased my knowledge of His Word. God's timing is perfect, he provided a way for me to get the studies I needed at home.

About the time I was finally comfortable praying and giving my parts in public, God was ready with another step for me. Sunday School teacher, Lois Cox, made the Bible come alive with her knowledge and expertise. One Sunday, she announced it was time to turn the class over to a younger teacher. "I have enjoyed teaching this class for several years," she said. "Now the time has come for me to step back and give someone else the opportunity to lead. Susie, I want you to teach this class the first Sunday of the month through the end of the year."

I believe when God led Linda and I to turn our exercise class into a Bible study class, he was preparing me for such a time as this.

28 - HOW SWEET IT IS

"Behold, how good and how pleasant it is for brethren to dwell together in unity!"
Psalm 133:1 (KJV)

Russell never doubted that God drew us together, though I'm sure he questioned his new bride's ideas from time to time. One way God chose to help our families get acquainted was in using our various talents and abilities to do projects.

I wasn't sure how much we could do with the parsonage without church permission. My creative mind desperately wanted to remodel the drab parsonage but hesitated to mention it. Eventually, me being me, I had to ask.

"Honey, the parsonage could use a bit of sprucing up here and there. Do you think it is okay if we wallpaper a little, at least the short wall in the living room around the fireplace? You can help me choose a nice design for the paper."

Russell tried to please when he could and quickly got the okay from the church trustees to go ahead with the project. Finding the right paper ended up being an all-day job. Without a doubt, our tastes were not the same; however, we finally found a beautiful pale gold print we both agreed on.

Although I asked for only one wall, we purchased several rolls of paper. I knew one wall would never be enough for me. Our entire family seemed eager to help. Some cut paper, some glued, some kept trash picked up and some "supervised". (No names here to protect the guilty.) We quickly papered the one wall. It was beautiful, but it seemed unfinished.

We continued with the same paper into the dining room and kitchen. Wow! Perfect!

Tired and hungry, we took a break to enjoy the pizzas Ricky and the guys made for us. I seem to remember smoke in the kitchen and darker-than-usual crust. Just saying! I also recall we ate all of it, whatever shape it was in.

The Rebel and Preacher Man

Later, with plenty of glue and ample supply of various wallpapers, we decided the master bathroom could use a little cheering up. At this point, I probably do not want to know what the church members were thinking about the new Mrs. Preach and her grandiose ideas.

Truly, it was not of real concern to me: Ingrained upon my heart forever is the memory of our families working together as we were getting to know each other. The laughter and stories told were unforgettable. God truly was molding our vastly different families together as only He could.

Much to our surprise, when the church realized the value of our improvements, they scheduled a workday to upgrade the bathrooms and do other needed work inside and out.

Speaking of outside, another fun workday occurred when son-in-law Tom brought his chain saw and tools to clear the low limbs and brush around the place. We all pitched in to stack branches and debris as we completely restored the beautiful corner lot.

For the first time in my life, I could truly enjoy the fruits of my labors. No one was going to complain because I didn't do it like they wanted. Neither would anyone make me pack up overnight, leave all behind and head to an unknown destination. I, too, had much to learn about family life, God's Family!

January - 1980
← 1st Anniversary -
Beefmaster's - Joplin, Mo.

3 December birthdays —

1983 ↗ Family Camping -
we visited each of
his former pastorates —

← PHOTOBOMBED!   MUCH LATER ↘

The best grandkids ever — at Great Grandma Kinslows —

29 - MEMORIAL DAY WITH OUR NEW FAMILY

"Precious in the sight of the Lord is the death of His saints."
Psalm 116:15 (KJV)

May 1979

With Memorial Day quickly approaching, it was back to the flower shop. It was another family project as we created elaborate wreaths and sprays to decorate our families' grave sites. This was to be a fun, learning time for us as we shared stories about our loved ones.

On a warm, sunny day, the Adams family packed a hefty picnic lunch and headed for the country. Our first stop was The Mound Cemetery not far from Joplin near the Kansas-Missouri state line. As we carefully laid flowers on graves, I told the kids about my first husband, Bob, and how he loved to trade cars and fish and sing. Nearby were the graves of Mother's parents and her little brother.

Next stop was back in Joplin at the beautiful Mount Hope Cemetery. This was my opportunity to hear from the children about their mother, Marcella. Though understandably a difficult time, it was also a time for us to rejoice knowing she had accepted Jesus as her Lord and Savior and was at home in Heaven.

Through the years, I came to know many of Marcella's family. Her brother, Marvin, was a member of Harmony Heights Baptist Church and often stopped by the house to have morning coffee. Her brother Mike, his wife Sharon, and their kids lived in St. Charles, Missouri and kept in close contact. In fact, we four adults often attended conferences together, and our families vacationed at each other's homes as I was readily accepted as family. When I married Preacher Man, I was blessed with more brothers and sisters than I could have ever asked for.

"Anyone up for a bit of ice cream or soda before we head to the woods?" We were all ready for a break and a change of subject for a bit.

Elsie: Tell me all about her!

Nellie: I am so happy for you!

Our First Mother's Day
MABEL BARTON
ELSIE ROSE
NELLIE BEENE
- 1979 -

Preacher Man — Loved on all week by his Three Sisters and a New Mother-in-law — WHAT A WEEK!

Rested and ready for more adventure, we headed south on 71 Highway. Following a quick tour of my hometown of Goodman, we stopped at Anderson Cemetery so I could tell them about my dad and several of his family. I regretted Michael and Laura did not get to know their grandpa; they would have loved his wild stories.

"Mom, this is right on the highway, not the woods. Is this our last stop?" I couldn't tell if they were ready for it to end, or if they were eager to go on.

The drive in the country to Price Cemetery was long and dusty as we crossed several little low-water bridges and followed dirt roads which seemed to have no end. No one ever knew how many wrong turns we made before we finally arrived at the cemetery. I am not sure I had ever driven there by myself before that day.

The redeeming quality for a long day was the journey home. First, we stopped at a lively stream to have lunch. Then Russell and the kids waded and splashed around in the cool water as I gathered up things and again counted my blessings.

This Memorial Day was a fun time; time to learn about our loved ones; time to enjoy our new family unit; and time to praise God for miraculously drawing us together.

30 - POKE GREENS AND BLACKBERRY BUSHES

"Every moving thing that liveth shall be meat for you; even as the green herb have I given you all things." Genesis 9:3 KJV

Exhausted, I plopped my tired body down in the nearest chair and surveyed the mess in front of me. It was our first summer, and I had cause to wonder what my family was thinking about their new mom by now.

I asked Russell if he liked poke greens. "Yes, I do," he replied quickly. "They are one of my favorites, especially picked fresh and cooked with bacon grease and onions!"

With his hearty approval, the kids and I headed to the country in search of poke greens. Spending time outside roaming the countryside with those little kids calling me "Mom" was my kind of day.

We shared the pastures with a cow now and then as we crossed more than one fence to gather our bounty. Tromping in the woods brought back sweet memories of my childhood. We laughed and talked and shared stories as we filled our bags.

After dinner, Michael and Laura showered and headed to bed leaving me to clean and prepare three huge trash bags packed full of poke greens. Three bags! What was I thinking? Who is going to eat that many greens?

I confess, as I began the third bag, I was quite intentional in culling the bad stuff. I mean, seriously, if a leaf was wrinkled, it got tossed! I was exhausted from the picking before beginning the cleaning process. In case you don't know, poke greens are not like apples or tomatoes or green beans. You cannot leave them a day or two until you have time and energy to work them up.

The Rebel and Preacher Man

That was our first and our last family poke green harvest. However, we did head to the woods again in the summer for wild blackberries. As I recall, we were gathering big berries and enjoying the chatter, until one or the other asked about the possibility of snakes in the bushes. That narrowed our search a bit. Again, it was a one-time experience. Nonetheless, priceless.

I will say, the entire family was more excited when I made fresh blackberry cobbler than they ever were staring at a big bowl of poke greens, with or without bacon.

***

While writing this chapter, I browsed through Russell's journal once again. In reply to the question, what did you do to make money as a child? He replied: "Sold poke greens for twenty cents a bag to buy school clothes."

Sold poke greens? SOLD poke greens? You can sell them? Oh, the dollars I threw away! In case you are wondering, the answer is "No, I am not heading for the pasture."

31 - MY STUBBORN WILL - GOD'S PATIENCE

"It shall come to pass that before they call, I will answer."
Isaiah 65:24 (KJV)

My first years in ministry were filled with new adventures apart from the local church. Russell was active in our local association, regional and state conventions, and conferences. I was eager to learn, to be a supportive mate, and desired to serve Jesus in every way. My deepest prayer on every new occasion was asking God to keep me teachable.

Prior to our marriage, the largest events I ever attended were in high school auditoriums. The first Missouri Baptist Convention and Evangelism Conference we attended together was overwhelming. There were more people in this huge venue than in my entire hometown. Not only that, but it seemed Preacher Man knew them all on a personal level.

We were seated in a huge sanctuary near the deaf section for the evangelism conference. As an enthusiastic interpreter signed "Amazing Grace", I was mesmerized. The respect and zeal of those who could not hear the music left me speechless as they lifted their hands and hearts in praises to their Savior and Lord.

Hour after hour, God showered His grace upon this new kid on the block as we journeyed through the day. By evening, our small motel room looked like a palace as I slipped my tired body into bed. A women's conference the next morning meant we needed to hit the road early.

***

What is Russell doing? Why is he not ready to go? Does he not remember the women's conference begins at 9:00 a.m.? We will be late. I told him we needed to be there early because I could not possibly make my way to the middle of a row. I might as well plan to go with him to his conferences. There will be plenty of room for me in the big auditorium.

"Here you are, Susie, right at the front door. I will park the car and go to my sessions. Don't worry, I will find you when our meetings are over." He continued with a smile, "Sorry we are a little late, but it will be fine."

Reluctantly, I got out of the car and closed the door. (Well, maybe I slammed it a bit.) It wasn't fine! We were very late, and the place was crowded! Several ladies were standing at the back searching desperately for empty seats.

Mumbling to myself, I reluctantly worked my way down the aisle toward the stage. I did not want to sit in the front! I needed to be in the back at the end of a row so I could scoot out of there when it was over.

This was not getting any better. As I approached the front, I was anticipating a long walk back to check out the balcony. And there it was. Most likely the only empty seat in the building. One seat! In the middle of the front row, facing the speaker.

As I quickly plopped myself down in the seat—my appointed seat—I wept! I confess, I cried! Two things not to miss. First, God saved me the best seat in the house. Secondly, it was in the first row because God knew I needed no distractions.

My hungry soul absorbed every word as author Evelyn Christenson expounded on her latest book entitled *What Happens When Women Pray.* I was sure my mother's and grandmothers' prayers through the years brought me back to God. I wanted to understand more about how to pray life-changing prayers for my family and my friends.

As always, God had more in store for me than I could ever comprehend. God opened opportunities for me to lead *What Happens When Women Pray* studies in several churches and small groups.

With each study, God stirred hearts of beloved faithful churchgoers like Janie S. At eighty-three she made her position clear from the beginning of our study. "I am taking this study because I believe in prayer and want to support this class. But do not ever ask me to pray out loud. I do not think it is necessary or something I should have to do." ("Hmm...where had I heard those words before")? With no provocation other than God's Holy Spirit, Janie soon volunteered to lead in prayer every Sunday for missionaries around the globe.

I will be forever thankful for a loving husband who carefully listened for God's Holy Spirit to speak to him before he listened to the impatient, know-it-all, rebel woman God gave him.

32 - UNDERSTANDING MY NEW WORLD

"Study to shew thyself approved unto God, a workman that needeth not to be ashamed, rightly dividing the word of truth."
2 Timothy 2:15 (KJV)

My parents did not attend church. Mother was either at work or busy weekends tending to Dad's parents in Southwest City or her parents in Joplin. Her strong faith was quite apparent, however, in the way she lived, dealt with people, and taught us kids. My earliest memories are of my brother Richard, and I being involved in children's church activities. As a youngster, I didn't know or care how churches were organized or why there were so many denominations. We attended every church in town regardless of the name on the door.

Because Russell was so involved in every aspect of local and state ministry, I got a crash course our first year of marriage. Harmony Heights Baptist Church was a member of the Southern Baptist and Missouri Baptist Conventions. I learned the state conventions were broken down into associations, either by county or regions. Several times a year we traveled throughout the state to conferences or retreats. (Did you notice the word 'traveled'? Isn't God good?)

Each association elected a Director of Missions (DOM) to lead their association. Harmony Heights Baptist Church belonged to the Spring River Baptist Association headquartered in Joplin, where T.O. Spicer served as the DOM. Of course, we attended the annual and quarterly business meetings, and supported as many training programs as our schedules allowed. T.O.'s wife, Martha, was what I call "altogether together". She was attractive, well-groomed, busy, talented, a good cook, musician, teacher, and on and on. Most of all, she made each individual feel God's love with her ready smile and servant attitude.

The association provided training events for music, Sunday School, discipleship, missions opportunities and leadership. I got a new appreciation for all those children's Vacation Bible Schools and camps I attended as a child. Each church in the association contributed money, personnel, and individualized training to make every event meaningful and affordable for all.

Pastor and wife fellowships at the local and state levels strengthened my faith. My, oh my, how pastors needed each other to stay strong and focused on God's plan for their family and their church. There was a bond, a trust developed quickly as they prayed and played together.

As I look back on my lifetime of shunning pastors, I have to laugh. Through the years as I became acquainted with those preacher guys, regardless of the size of their ministries, the more I realized how God surely calls each one. I believe He looks down from Heaven on a bunch of little boys at play and says, "See little Russell over there? And Ron and Danny and Terry? I will stir those little boys' hearts toward preaching the gospel. To survive at all, they will definitely need a church full of praying mothers and grandmothers to keep them on the straight and narrow." After 40 plus years of ministry, I believe it still!

Seriously, I learned to have the utmost respect and honor for those whom God has called into the ministry. Russell never lost the awe of being given the task to lead a congregation to follow Jesus. When asked to consider being a DOM, he had only one reply: "No. Definitely not. God called me to pastor, and I won't give that up."

It pleased me to hear him say that because this country gal was definitely no Martha Spicer.

OLD FASHIONED REVIVALS

33 - SAYING GOODBYE AND MOVING ON

"Have I not commanded you? Be strong and of good courage; do not be afraid, nor be dismayed, for the Lord your God is with you wherever you go."
Joshua 1:9 (NKJV)

October 1982

Harmony Heights Baptist Church had grown as Russell continued his strong messages on the realities of sin, hell, and Jesus Christ as the only answer to man's problems.

Moving was not on my radar at all when a group of visitors showed up on Sunday morning for worship. They quickly found seats and sat in a huddle near the front of the sanctuary. Russell informed me before the service a Pastor Search Committee from Miami, Oklahoma was there to visit with him about becoming their pastor.

Mixed emotions kept me from hearing his message as I entertained the thoughts of moving. Harmony Heights was family; we belonged here. Michael and Laura would have to change schools. We would be farther from Mother and my family. Do I get a vote on this? I've moved enough in one lifetime; do I really have to move again?

Little did I know this was the first of many search committees as the Lord moved us out of our comfort zones and into new areas of ministry for His Kingdom. I quickly learned to trust God with the smallest details when He was directing the move.

A family of five came forward to join the church as others prayed at the altar during the invitation. My heart was questioning what took place. Was this a sign we were to stay? Or was God saying He could take care of the church if He called us away?

Several interviews followed before Russell preached a challenging morning message for Southern Hills Baptist Church in Miami, Oklahoma. A lengthy question and answer session lasted most of the afternoon. That evening after his message, he was extended a 100% call to become their pastor. It was a beautiful church on a corner lot with well cared for grounds. Inside the sanctuary, the pale blue walls and white ceiling sported beautiful chandeliers and elaborate furnishings.

With no parsonage ready to move into, we searched for a home near the school which was adequate for our family. We found a two-story house with bedrooms for everyone and a craft/flower room for me.

The most exciting time in any ministry is to witness someone surrender their life to Jesus. Opal Harp was one such lady. She lived alone in a clean, but cluttered little house. Responding to her call one evening, Russell and I had the privilege to kneel with her as she tearfully asked Jesus into her heart. "Glory! Glory!" she yelled as tears flowed furiously down her wrinkled cheeks and onto the floor. She was aged and could barely stand on her own, yet she faithfully made her way to the church altar to pray for friends and family to know her Jesus. The story never gets old!

During our years there, at least five men felt God's call to preach and were ordained and sent out by the church. God called several to serve as deacons, many others as first-time teachers and leaders. New ministries began for children and for adults as the church continued to grow.

While our ministry there bore much fruit, it was obvious we were a bit too casual to suit a few people. Preacher Man simply said we all need to be reminded from time to time a church is a body of baptized believers with Christ as the head. Sometimes as God's children, we misbehave. As we learn to keep our focus on Jesus and not our issues, He will make our paths straight. God has reminded me often; His ways are not my ways and I need to back off and let Him handle situations that trouble me.

Sometimes I listened, at other times....

34 - GOD BLESSES SUSIE'S FLOWERS

"You shall eat the fruit of the labor of your hands; you shall be blessed, and it shall be well with you." Psalm 128:2 (ESV)

As our ministries in Oklahoma flourished, so did our extra income opportunities. I slowly eased out of the home remodeling business after we wed and focused more on flowers and crafts. This was not only good for extra income, but it also opened areas of ministry to women and girls I had not expected.

Preacher Man was not too interested in helping me with crafts. His idea of a hobby was to read a book, take a walk, or to sit and chat with any who would listen. However, he loved people whatever their age, was a magnificent talker, and a great salesman; his encouragement refreshed my soul and pushed me to do better.

Corsages were still popular in the early eighties, especially adorning a lady's Sunday best. When we pastored at Harmony Heights, I created silk corsages for all the ladies on the first Mother's Day after I joined the church. Surprisingly, this rapidly generated requests for arrangements for homes and special occasions. While in Joplin, God formed forever friendships through families like Sue Walter and her girls as we searched my flower bins together. These bonding opportunities flourished wherever we were called to serve.

Russell always managed to mention his wife's beautiful flowers when he counseled engaged couples. If I did the wedding flowers, young couples were free to come to our home anytime with suggestions or simply to watch the progress. Russell invariably planned to be home if at all possible. Only God could provide such a casual setting to open such deep spiritual conversations. Their eager ears and hearts took in every word as did the ears of their florist.

1984 - Vinita, Oklahoma -
Making Grapevine Wreaths

1994
Rohnert Park,
California -
Washing
Little Furry
Bears Eyes

1977 - Mothers Day -
Claremore, Oklahoma -
Mother selling
Feather Flowers
at Walmart -

All in the Family

The Rebel and Preacher Man

Through our many moves, flowers and crafts played a big role both in providing extra income as well as natural witnessing opportunities. In Miami, Oklahoma, I created colorful sprays and containers for Decoration Day. About mid-May, Russell and Michael loaded the truck and headed for a vacant lot on busy Steve Owens Blvd. I remained at home and continued making more sprays. Teenage Michael enjoyed driving back and forth periodically to restock.

We joined a barter group in Miami which expanded our inventory. One of the first big projects we undertook required our entire family working together. We desperately needed Russell and Michael's manpower and Laura's creative expertise to tackle this one.

The project was to decorate a new fitness center, in particular the pool and exercise areas. This meant artificial trees and greenery, wreaths, and appropriate floral enhancements. This project, several open houses for realty companies plus refurbishment of a local restaurant built our barter dollars rapidly.

During the same time, Massa's Distributing Company in Joplin suffered a fire in their warehouse, leaving them with crates of smoked milk glass bud vases. We purchased the vases for pennies on the dollar and spent weeks scrubbing off the smoke. Eventually, we owned cases of beautiful vases to use and to run through the barter system. A lot of tedious work really paid off in the end.

Earned barter dollars enabled us to get dental work and vision care for the family, tires and major car repairs, restaurant and gas cards, and several wonderful family trips. Working together as a family with what was available to us, God blessed our efforts in a mighty way.

In the fall, it was back to the woods to gather grapevines. Russell's sisters stood and watched in awe as we dumped truckloads of grapevines in the yard and rolled them into wreaths. They had cause to wonder about their little brother and his crazy young bride. We all knew the truth of the matter: his major contribution to the project was not in being the salesman. He relished the opportunity to tell every customer about Jesus as he peddled our wares.

35 - WE'RE MOVING WHERE?

"Be very careful, then, how you live-not as unwise but as wise, making the most of every opportunity, because the days are evil. Therefore, do not be foolish, but understand what the Lord's will is." Ephesians 5:15-17 (NIV)

Preaching revivals fed Russell's passion for winning souls to Jesus. In the few years we had been married, he led revivals in Illinois, Louisiana, and California, as well as across Missouri. The churches and pastors he served in this way were encouraged by his ministry. His greatest joy was leading souls to a saving faith in Jesus Christ. Not one to complain, I'm sure it was difficult for him to preach Sunday after Sunday to the same people with little or no public decisions made.

While we were in Miami, Rev. Jim Davis invited Russell to preach a revival in southern California. The Davis and Adams families met in the seventies in Clinton, Missouri where Russell pastored Northeast Baptist Church. A deacon invited Jim to Northeast by telling him he didn't love his children very much if he wasn't taking them to church. Jim and Dorothy and their children not only attended, but Jim loved the pastor on their first visit, and they joined and began serving in the church. Dorothy tells me they not only respected him as pastor; they admired Russell and Marcella for fostering Debbie and adopting Michael and Laura. Russell had the joy of ordaining Jim to preach the gospel. Through the years, the two families built strong friendships. With great confidence in his ability to preach strong evangelistic messages, Jim invited Russell to lead his revivals often.

Evangelistic preachers were few and far between in California. People from surrounding churches flocked to First

Baptist Church, Lake Elsinore to hear a country preacher boldly proclaim God's word. Several members of nearby Lakeview Southern Baptist Church were in attendance every night. Bill and Marie Carter and Ben Floyd were particularly enamored by the strong, evangelistic messages and people coming forward in each service to be saved, pray, or join the church.

Within a few weeks of Russell's return home, he began getting calls from the Lakeview Church, particularly from Marie Carter. Her frequent calls became an area of concern for our family. Moving across the state line into Oklahoma was one thing; moving to the west coast was quite another. Every summer we invited our grandchildren to our home for a week of Vacation Bible School; how could I ever give up those times with our family?

Then there was my mother. More than likely, she would think her gypsy daughter encouraged the move since I had always wanted to go to California. I could not imagine what it would be like for Russell to have to tell his sisters and brothers he was leaving. From the world's standpoint, we had cause to wonder if God would have us make such a drastic move.

Complicating the issue was the fact of the B.F. Goodrich plant in Miami closing. Miami, Oklahoma was a small town of 15,000 residents and 1,900 of them were losing their jobs. Three hundred families immediately relocated to another Goodrich plant. The entire town was hurt and needed a strong Christian witness as they struggled to hang on to their community and rebuild.

As our family continued to pray and seek God's will, it became clear God's plan for us was to move to California. One of the more difficult considerations was our two teenagers.

The Rebel and Preacher Man

Michael and Laura lived in Joplin for about five years before our move to Oklahoma. Nevertheless, both seemed to enjoy their new youth groups, camps, and other activities while in Oklahoma. Michael entered college in Miami and chose to stay in Oklahoma when we moved again. Laura was in her senior year in high school. Should she stay with someone in Miami, or move with us? We later learned how God was in the process of fulfilling the dreams of a young girl in ways we could not imagine.

"I'll go wherever you go, Preacher Man"

36 - SOUTHERN CALIFORNIA HERE WE COME

"Walk in obedience to all that the Lord your God has commanded you, so that you may live and prosper and prolong your days in the land that you will possess." Deuteronomy 5:33 (NIV)

January 1986

We left Oklahoma the day after Christmas and arrived in California in time to unpack a few things and attend our first Watch Night Party at Lakeview First Baptist Church.

The difference in God's economy and man's is never so clear as when there is a job change. In the secular world, one seeks a larger paycheck, bigger home, and more benefits. In ministry, the priority is clearly hearing God's call and trusting Him to meet the needs. We left our own house for a tiny trailer on a fenced, sandy lot by the church. My view of sprawling oaks and green valleys gave way to a few tall palms and sand.

On the positive side, a storage shed by the parsonage served well as a flower shop. Along one fence were grape vines producing huge clumps of grapes each year. I learned to love this new country as I spent early mornings on the deck with the Lord... With Bible in one hand and fresh grapes in the other, I praised God for the snowy San Bernardino Mountain Range towering high above our palm trees.

The peace of knowing we were where God wanted us to be outweighed the struggles. God blessed Russell's strong, evangelistic preaching. Our building skills came in handy as we turned a small trailer into classes for nursery and preschoolers of our growing Young Adult classes.

First Baptist Church - Lakeview, CA -

- BAPTISED -
Dan Young & Grandsons

Valentine Banquet - serenaded by Russell Rhoda

"Little Puppy" I kept for a friend!

ZING

Laura settled into Hemet High School where there was 500 in her graduating class. It surely was a difficult time for her although she never complained. It was comforting for her to have old family friends, Jim and Dorothy Davis take her to Denny's to celebrate her graduation. Through a work program at school, she got a job at JC Penney's Department Store. She felt right at home when she was assigned to dress and display mannequins throughout the store.

Laura had a phenomenal way with children and befriended a young Down's Syndrome girl in our neighborhood. As Laura spent time with young Cathy and gained her trust, she was able to teach her how to write her name and make pictures and cards. God's pure love shown through them as they laughed and worked together.

We quickly became friends with a family who lived across the road from the church. Dian Ferris and her children were attending Lakeview Church regularly. There was clearly more on her mind than flowers when she dropped by after church. Dian confessed she really needed to talk to the pastor. She invited Jesus into her heart that day to forgive her sins and become the lord of her life. Later, some of her children followed. Although her husband, Pete, never made a habit of coming to church, he often relaxed outside on the porch during services. He was always ready to donate his time, tools, and expertise when the church needed painting or repaired.

Dian did couponing, purchasing household products for pennies on the dollar. Pete bought containers of seconds or damaged goods to recycle. Their entire family was involved in selling at flea markets. Pete took a liking to Russell and invited him to help sell his wares. Once a week my sleepyhead hubby left at 5:00 am for a busy Los Angeles Flea Market. The four of us spent several hours a week in their home refurbishing products. Our workday often ended with Pete grilling steaks and preparing a feast.

The Rebel and Preacher Man

Bill and Marie Carter became close friends as well, though Marie and I struggled with a few control issues. She was so like my mother in many ways. Often Bill and I sat back and watched Marie and the pastor work out their disagreements. I, on the other hand, let things sit on the back burner and simmer while I smiled and went about my business.

For two years I sold Home Interiors and Gifts in people's homes on a party plan. One week I would be in an elaborate home in Indio's desert, and the next in a Hispanic complex in busy Santa Ana. When I think now of where I boldly took my little Mercury Lynx all alone, I praise God for His unending care for me. There was only one night Russell insisted on going with me. As God is my witness, that was the night the timing chain went out on the car while we were driving on the inside lane of busy Santa Ana Freeway. Two vehicles following directly behind us miraculously slowed down and eased into the next lane allowing us to safely coast our way off the exit ramp.

You know without me saying, there "just happened" to be a mall area and garage open near the off ramp. With Russell with me, we could leave the vehicle there and call the host to come get us so I could do the show. After the show, we were taken to a motel near the garage where we enjoyed the evening and a free breakfast in the morning. We praised God for His care as we headed home with a repaired vehicle. I often wonder how many times God had rescued us when we weren't even aware we needed to be protected. I shudder to think how it could have played out without Preacher Man by my side. I praise Him daily for His watch care over this rebel.

Another praise here: Among other prizes, my sales earned me a trip to Dallas, Texas, home of Mary Crowley, creator of

Home Interiors and Gifts. Corrie ten Boom stayed in Mary's home at one time when she was ill. An undeniable Presence of God's Spirit hovered over a beautiful, tiny room overlooking a lovely prayer garden. My prize wasn't in winning the trip however, it was in how a gracious God let me sense the Holy Spirit's presence in a real and powerful way.

We remained active in local association and state-wide functions wherever we lived. He made sure I never missed a ladies' event anywhere in the state. In each church, God led me to begin a weekly LIFT Bible Study and Prayer class for women and girls. At the same time, Russell worked diligently to find ways to encourage the men and boys in their ministries.

We missed our family terribly. One of the most difficult times was not being able to attend Michael and Diane's wedding.

I was extremely thankful to know Rick escorted my beautiful mother to his brother's wedding. In addition, this was the first year for a Vacation Bible School without having our grandkids stay with us for the week. It was heart wrenching. Yet, through it all, God was indeed blessing our faithfulness to His call.

At the same time, Laura got to fulfill a

The Rebel and Preacher Man

lifelong dream of attending the Fashion Institute of Design and Merchandising (FIDM), a private college in downtown Los Angeles. You see, we did not know she longed to go to this school to study. It must have seemed an impossible dream for a little girl in faraway Oklahoma to go to school in Los Angeles. But Laura's Loving Father heard her simple prayers and answered her request in a way none of us could comprehend. Now, with her family serving a church a couple of hours from Los Angeles, Laura was able to be home many weekends and in the summer.

For the rebel, I could grab my camera and find enough to keep my traveling spirit tamed for sure. My choices for a day away were unlimited. A shopping trip to Palm Springs? A day of writing in the secluded mountains? Pick up shells along the ocean's sandy beaches? Explore some venues in Los Angeles? Stock up food at the fresh fruit markets? Go treasure hunting in acres of swap meets? The list is endless and Preacher Man was always willing to hand me the keys and let me have my "Susie Day."

37 - I WASN'T EXPECTING THIS

"This God, His way is perfect; the promise of the Lord proves true. He is a shield for all who take refuge in Him."
2 Samuel 22:31 (RSV)

From our first meeting twenty years earlier, I had complete confidence in Russell as my pastor. It never waned. I knew God directed his messages; I observed too many lives changed through his faithful preaching of God's Word.

I rarely knew what Russell was going to preach about on Sunday morning. He said he didn't always know either as God sometimes prompted him to change his message at the last minute. And so it was: on a Sunday morning at Lakeview Southern Baptist Church, he boldly preached a message from Acts chapter 19 instead of his prepared Old Testament message.

We had never talked about my conversion or baptism, so he had no inkling of my life-long struggle with people in today's world who felt the need to be baptized a second time. The account in Acts was different because those people recognized that Jesus, the promised Messiah, was now with them.

Later at home, my entire day was shot as I pondered the scripture in relation to my own testimony. I recalled my salvation experience. Under conviction as a young, struggling teen, a close friend took me to her pastor's home to talk about my relationship with Jesus Christ. I clearly remember kneeling by his old brown couch and asking Jesus to come into my heart and forgive my sins. God's perfect love, peace, and joy filled my soul.

The Rebel and Preacher Man

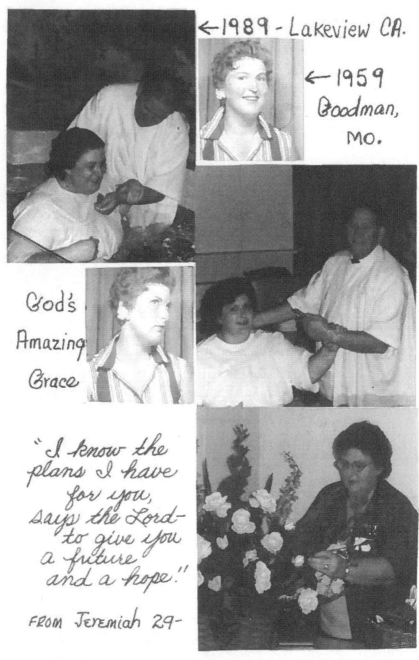

I never doubted my salvation. Even in what I call my wandering years, I knew I was a child of God. His Holy Spirit tugged at my heart unmercifully, especially when I was in trouble. The truth is, I would repent and earnestly vow to follow Jesus. Of course, as the storm blew over, I slipped back to my sinful, self-centered ways.

As the years passed, God's Holy Spirit continued to gently tug on my heart strings. I knew something was amiss but couldn't reconcile it with my rebel nature. After all, I knew for sure I was a Christian. Why was I still uneasy?

As time passed, it became clear my earlier baptism in the river as a young child was years before I was saved. My brother told me a group of us went forward in a revival and later were all baptized together. I did not remember anyone talking to me individually, although they may have.

God helped me see, through the message that morning, I had not been scripturally baptized after my salvation experience in that preacher's home. Even understanding the truth, I continued to struggle. Why should it matter now? I knew I was God's child. Besides, no one in California knew the difference. God spoke His message quite clearly to this stubborn rebel that Sunday: "I know, and I care. I want you to obey me."

Imagine being the pastor when your wife comes bawling down the aisle on Sunday night. "You have to baptize me!" Wanting to make it perfectly clear it was God who changed the direction of his morning message, he later told me he almost ignored the Holy Spirit's prompting and preached the message he prepared earlier. As I look back, I'm quite sure the devil was trying his best to discourage him from following the "still small voice" in his heart.

A week later he baptized me alright – in cold water. He insisted he did not fill the baptistry full because I was short and

The Rebel and Preacher Man

did not require all that water. No one told him the heater would not work until the baptistry was completely full. I can still feel the icy water going up my spine as he dunked me. Maybe God wanted to be sure I remembered the occasion.

The complete peace which enveloped me when I finally surrendered my all to my Lord and Savior, Jesus Christ, is with me still. I learned right away, whatever issue is puzzling a child of God is important, no matter how trivial we try to make it. It is a big thing if it hinders our personal walk with Jesus in any way. Complete freedom in Jesus—you can't explain it. You must live it.

38 - PREACHER MAN – FOREVER LEARNING

"Study to shew thyself approved unto God, a workman that needeth not to be ashamed, rightly dividing the word of truth."
2 Timothy 2:15 (KJV)

As a new Christian in his thirties, Russell surrendered his life for special service. He got his GED and began preparing for the future. He and Marcella quit their jobs, sold their home, and moved to Missouri where he entered Hannibal LaGrange College to prepare for ministry. At the age of 39, he was referred to as the 'old man' on campus. He graduated Hannibal LaGrange in 1965.

Continuing his studies, he entered Northeast Missouri State University in Kirksville. He obtained master's degree in theology and history in 1987. He received an Honorary Doctor of Divinity degree from International Bible Institute and Seminary. In Spring River Baptist Association, Joplin, he accumulated eight hours of Seminary Extension credit.

Now, although in his sixties and thinking he may have only a few years left to pastor, he felt a need for more structured studies and began some correspondence classes. He signed up for classes through Faith College and Seminary in Anderson, South Carolina. I can still hear his firm comments when he was told the school may not be recognized in Southern Baptist circles. "This is not for them; it is for me personally. I am concerned about keeping my mind sharp. This school provides the subjects I feel I need, and with God's help, I plan to give it my best. We must never, ever quit studying His Word."

The Rebel and Preacher Man

As time permitted, day after day, week after week, when the breakfast table was cleared, out came his books. He found it harder to keep at it than he did in earlier years, but he was determined this was God's plan for him. Fortunately, he married a secretary-on-call eager to type all his papers. Not only was it an honor, but it also became a learning experience for me as well. I was so proud of him and his determination to follow God's leading.

In 1989 we drove to South Carolina for his graduation. Good friends, Joe and Jane Hurst were living in the state and able to celebrate with us. (Joe surrendered to the ministry under Russell's pastorate in Oklahoma and served with us and Jim and Dorothy Davis in California.) Handsome Preacher Man looked like a tower of strength in his cap and gown. However, I watched his tightly-clasped hands behind his back nervously twitch as he waited his turn to get his much-deserved diploma.

At a beautiful, formal reception, his wife practically lost it. Already caught up in the emotion of the day, a young man presented a Ray Boltz song I had never heard before. *"Thank you, for giving to the Lord, I was a life that was changed...."* By God's grace and a stiff upper lip, I remained calm and humbled as I reflected on the lives God allowed us to touch.

The hours my husband struggled to complete these courses was definitely not for the degree. He never wanted to be called "Doctor Adams." For Russell, it was the burning desire in his spirit to know more about his Savior and how to better serve Him. He held an Honorary Doctorate already so for good friends like the Carters, two degrees meant he was now "Doctor, Doctor!"

After a long day at a state convention, I was ready to turn in. Preacher Man, on the other hand, was in his pajamas, writing out his thankfulness to God and to the churches he served. He had dropped out of high school to join the army. Yet, while he was a married man in his thirties, God had moved mountains for him so he could continue his education. His lifetime goal now was to prepare for the ministry. He never lost his sense of awe that God would use him.

The stories are endless of how God used a humble high school drop-out to impact families for eternity. One such family at Lakeview First Baptist was Dan and June Young. June prayed for her husband and children and grandchildren for years. I can still hear her joyful "amen" as her husband accepted Jesus as His Savior and Lord. Russell got to baptize Dan along with his two grandsons. What a drastic change this made in the Young family as Dan began boldly witnessing to all within his hearing.

The list goes on and on, in every church we served, God blessed His faithful servant's ministry. Russell's secret was simple: keep the main thing the main thing: Jesus saves!

39 - THE REBEL RETURNS

"Set a guard, O Lord, over my mouth; Keep watch over the door of my lips."
Psalm 141:3 (KJV)

"Marie, the pastor's already at the front of the line. You go ahead and begin; I'll be back soon." I was firm, but polite.

"Susie," she replied gruffly. "You have to go to the front of the line with your husband so we can eat!" She insisted on having her way.

Russell had preached his last message at Lakeview First Baptist Church that morning. The next day we were to load our final belongings onto the moving van and leave the beautiful desert to begin a pastorate north of San Francisco. God richly blessed our Lakeview ministry both numerically and spiritually. We made lifetime friends there; emotions were mixed as we prepared to leave.

Beautifully decorated tables were laden with Bro. Russell's favorite foods; it was a banquet fit for a king. Moving day is a bittersweet time for the pastor and family as well as for the congregation.

Smiling slightly, I tried to be calm. "Marie, it's going to be okay. Start without me. I will be back as soon as I can. Sue loaned me her video camera to take a few pictures before we leave. I will miss the desert, orange groves, sheep, and palm trees."

***

Bill and Marie became close friends of ours during the five years we served there. She was instrumental in calling Russell as pastor and moving us from Oklahoma to California. The four of us were always ready to head to a gospel sing or revival in the area. And as traditional Baptists, we knew all the good places to eat. Yes, together we enjoyed many good times and victories. But it was clear from day one Marie kept a watchful eye on "her church" and made sure everything was done properly and in order.

Anyone else could have asked me to get in line with my husband and I most likely would have done so. At the very least, I would have declined more gracefully. But the rebel inside me decided Marie was not winning this war, not this time. The more I tried to decline, the more she insisted! "Susie, get up there where you belong."

Marie was the size of my mother, about the same age, and even the same shade of red hair sprinkled with a touch of gray. To me, her tone of voice when she didn't get her way sounded exactly like Mother when she was riled. The entire church knew Marie insisted on having the final word, especially in the kitchen. All those years I managed to keep my cool. But this time, all I could hear was Mother's voice giving me orders.

Holding my ground, I quickly snapped back at her. "Marie, I'm not going to get in line now. I have other things to do." One word led to another, and we ended up in the kitchen having it out. All the bitterness, anger, and withheld conversations I wanted to have with my mom or Marie came pouring out before I could stop. Marie's husband, Bill, peeked in the kitchen, turned around, and quickly walked away. As did my precious husband. I'm sure there was a lot of praying going on!

I grabbed Sue's camera and headed off in the car to take pictures. Lunch was not on my agenda. I don't know whether Marie ate or not. As you might suspect, she did not come to help load the truck the next day or say goodbye as we left town.

I'd like to tell you I felt so sorry the incident happened at all. I would like you to hear me say I yelled, "Stop the car! I have to go back and fix this. I'm so, so sorry!" I would like to tell you it happened, and we hugged and made up right then and there. I could tell you that. You might even believe it and never know the difference. But I would know.

It didn't happen. Not at all. This volcano had been simmering in me since childhood. The final eruption was hot and wicked. It hit unintended places and hurt more people than the two of us. It left a scar on my soul. I do not ever want it to happen again to me or to anyone else.

As we packed to leave the next day, no one mentioned the incident. We got hugs and good wishes from the crew that loaded our things. Tenderhearted Bill was kind; even giving us both hugs as we left. Although I missed Marie, anger, bitterness, and selfish pride still had a hold on me.

As we passed Los Angeles and headed north, my desire to travel consumed my thoughts as my confrontation with Marie took a back seat.

40 - HAPPY TRAVELERS ON THE ROAD AGAIN

"For by one Spirit we were all baptized into one body, whether Jews or Greeks, whether slaves or free, and we were all made to drink of one Spirit."
1 Corinthians 12:13 (NKJV)

March 1991

The drive up 101 Highway along California's beautiful coast was breathtaking. San Francisco was a bit of a challenge in places, but we expected it. What we could not have expected is all God had prepared for us in northern California. Excitement built as we crossed the massive Golden Gate Bridge, waving to our Southern Baptist Golden Gate Seminary as we headed north toward Rohnert Park.

The call to serve this church was a miracle in and of itself. Seven people of various ages and nationalities formed the Pastor Search Committee for Rohnert Park First Baptist Church. The size of the church's congregation, exceptional facilities and proximity to the seminary meant there had been an enormous stack of applicants from which to choose. We were told that, mainly because of his age, Russell's resume kept getting moved to the bottom of the stack. Therefore, when his call was unanimous, we knew without a doubt it was God's plan. One young man said, "God always gets His way in spite of us!"

The church did not own a parsonage, so they paid a housing allowance and let the pastor find a suitable home. Members Chuck and Marsha Hinaman took us right in as family and guided our search. We not only found a nice home, but we also enjoyed the personal tour of our new area.

The Rohnert Park church was an active congregation with Children's, Youth, and Adult Ministries, a Special Education

Class, Hispanic and Chinese Ministries, and ongoing soul-winning classes. Somewhere in my "stack of stuff", I have a priceless video of this church's presentation of The Last Supper. Pastor Russell portrayed Jesus washing the disciples' feet with several nationalities and ages participating in the drama. Dare to imagine what our home in Heaven will be like when all God's children are truly one.

Before we were completely moved in, Russell had an issue he wanted addressed immediately. The beautifully appointed sanctuary sported a large secretary's office and storage room to the left of the baptistry. To the right was the pastor's study and a spacious counseling area. The door leading to one of the changing rooms for the baptistry was nailed shut. "Before I preach my first sermon on Sunday, I want both entries opened, and a stack of towels put in each room. We are here to win souls to Jesus Christ, and nothing more," Russell declared. And God honored the church. Quite often the Hispanic and Chinese congregations had candidates for baptism right along with ours. What a beautiful picture of God's love as our families joined in worship together.

It was sometimes difficult to verbally understand many in Charlene Bell's large Special Education class; however, their smiles were infectious. As her class took their turn in filling the choir in the summer, it was humbling. Their sweet faces bubbled with pride and joy as they loudly belted out their rendition of "Jesus Loves Me". I believe they understood Jesus' love more than most of us. Laura quickly became involved in our church, leading the youth, playing the piano, and other ministries. Nearby Mt. Gilead Bible Conference initially hired Laura to help in the kitchen and bakery. After seeing her interaction with the students, she was asked to be Youth Activity Director.

Teaching the Young Adult Sunday School class at Rohnert Park is one of the highlights of my personal ministries. Many came into my class from unchurched backgrounds, accepted Jesus, and were on fire. One Sunday morning, a new couple came to our class because Grandpa had insisted they take their young son to church. When the eager young father began interrupting the lesson with simple questions, my young adults were armed and ready. I sat back and watched as God took over and grew those young people into bold witnesses. Thoughts of how complacent we have become back in the Bible Belt burdened my heart. It was refreshing to observe the confidence of these young adults.

When Deacon Steve White refurbished a computer for us (our first one), Russell's secretary, Ruth Barnett, offered to teach Pastor how to use it, but he declined. He was content to spread the gospel message and let me learn the techie stuff. In every church he pastored, I eventually did the church brochures and newsletters filled with newsy articles and drawings. Thank you, Goodman High School, for the training!

I've often said, "God never wastes anything". It's so very true; the computer opened a whole new world of ministry opportunities for us. So, too, did a quilting class June Timian insisted I take. I was right proud of my finished project; a beautiful wall hanging with tiny, even stitches. Little did I know where this new appreciation of quilting would lead when we eventually moved back home to Missouri.

41 - LIFT CLASS LESSON CONVICTS TEACHER

"Let the word of Christ dwell in you richly in all wisdom."
Colossians 3:16a (KJV)

I was greatly honored to lead LIFT (Ladies In Fellowship Together) classes at Joplin's Harmony Heights Baptist Church, and to begin the program in various other churches. As we moved from Missouri to Oklahoma to southern California, I led in women's ministries and LIFT classes in every church we served.

In Rohnert Park FBC, we planned a two-day ladies' retreat at Lord's Land, Mendocino, originally home to the hippies in the sixties. The owner became a radical Christian, renamed her huge house and cabins "The Lord's Land" and hosted Biblical retreats. The property was adorned with huge wooden scripture signs, prayer gardens, and wildlife. Our main sessions were in the big house where deer roamed outside as we worshiped. The ocean and shopping were a few miles away.

We began two LIFT Classes a week to accommodate different age groups and work schedules. Each class often began with Evelyn Christiansen's book "What Happens When Women Pray" followed by a book of the Bible or character study however God led. In one class at Rohnert Park, our ladies delved into a familiar study of Colossians. As often happens, God prepared a surprising lesson for Teacher (me).

In chapter one, Paul encourages believers, prays for them, and elaborates on what it means to follow Christ with your whole heart. Paul is showing unconditional love and concern for a church he most likely never visited. He was thankful for their faith in Christ and love for one another. As I led, my heart filled with joy, thankfulness, and love for fellow Christians.

Moving to chapter two, Paul stresses the unity and strength that comes naturally through the mystery of following Christ. He challenges them to walk in Christ, to trust only in Him for strength and direction.

The classes were certainly anointed by God; only He could identify and meet the needs of each heart as we studied and prayed together week after week.

Chapter three caught me totally off guard. My confidence was high as we discussed being raised with Christ and seeking those things which were above. I was God-conscious, focused on things above, and listened carefully for His still small voice. I felt secure in putting off the old man full of deceit, wrath, malice, lying, blasphemy.

Once we put off the old man, we are admonished in verses twelve and following to put on the new man. Our traits should show Jesus Christ. As the discussions centered on putting on love, kindness, tender mercies, and gentleness God unexpectedly struck a chord in my heart.

As if written in big red letters on my page, these words from chapter three spoke directly to my spirit... *"bearing with one another, and forgiving one another, if anyone has a complaint against another; even as Christ forgave you, so you also **must do**."*

By God's grace alone, I made it through the class, but in the car the floods came. By the time I reached home, I was in such a mess my poor husband was at a loss as to what to do with me. "What in the world happened to you? Are you okay? Do you need a doctor? What can I do?"

"It was our Bible study." The tears would not stop as I

The Rebel and Preacher Man

continued. "We have to go back to Lakeview when we can. I need to talk to Marie."

And return we did. My patient husband was keenly aware of how much this incident strained the beautiful relationship we both enjoyed with the Carters. I needed to personally see her, hug her, ask her to forgive me, tell her how much I loved her. God granted Marie and I and our families a remarkable time of forgiveness and healing.

Dear Reader, whatever situation you are in, no matter who has wronged you or you them, stay in God's Word. In His timing, when your heart is ready, He will direct you. The joy and peace which comes from listening to God and following Him in every decision you make will take you places spiritually and physically beyond anything you could imagine or hope for.

42 - MINISTERING THROUGH CRAFTS

"Sing to the Lord, for he has done wonderful things. Make known his praise around the world." Isaiah 12:5 (NASB)

After the house we lived in was suddenly put up for sale, we were invited by an elderly couple to help them find a house for an investment. The church could then rent it from them for a parsonage. Wow! Looking at homes for sale instead of rent made all the difference. How fun! We settled on a beautiful two-story home with a four-car garage that had never housed a vehicle. The down payment was sixty thousand dollars. Sixty thousand dollars! At that time, one could buy a nice home in Missouri, furnish it, and most likely have a bit left for a vehicle with only her down payment.

The home itself was magnificent. There were several rooms upstairs, a beautiful landing and curved stairs coming down into the living room. We hosted more events there than any place we lived. The garage was made-to-order for a crafter with floor to ceiling shelves along two walls, space for several worktables and desks, and a beautiful open space for a showroom. I much preferred peddling my wares to office work so this was made to order.

Early one morning, Laura, Dorothy Davis and I bravely headed to downtown San Francisco's wholesale marketplace. Dropping Laura off on a corner to shop at some kiosks, we agreed on a time to pick her up in the same place.

"No problem, if you aren't here, I'll call Dad."

"No, Honey! No! No! No! Do not call your dad. You wait right here; we'll be here to get you."

The Rebel and Preacher Man

I drove the car a little closer to the crowded market area and felt blessed to find a parking place close to our shopping destination. Dorothy and I quickly perused several warehouses: As we returned with our bounty and neared our parking space, we saw my car being towed away! In my haste, I unknowingly had parked in a "No Parking" zone. After a six-block-long walk and a bit poorer, we claimed our vehicle and rushed to pick up my brave daughter. Remember, this was before cell phones; it was a happy time.

The good news was our shelves were stacked high with a gross each of several size bears and other treasures. Even Preacher Man got into the act when his busy schedule permitted. He helped Laura fluff each bear, wiping the fur away from their eyes with a wet cloth. We filled our "Hugs from the Heart" shop with honey bears, Shop-Til-You-Drop bears, bunnies, burlap cows and more. I made prairie dolls out of embroidered pillowcases and men's white hankies, and, of course, flower creations and greeting cards.

My talented daughter, salesman husband, and I loaded our van once a week for the Santa Rosa Street Market: Five downtown blocks were closed to traffic as vendors lined both sides of the street. A big seller was Laura's quillows (quilts which folded into a pillow).

Steve and Sheri White were instrumental in helping our craft business flourish. Frequently, Steve stopped by on his way to work to get a gift for someone in his office. Sheri and I often set up on Friday and Saturday at area craft fairs. Jim and Dorothy Davis (now pastoring in nearby Napa Valley) also brought a line of crafts and set up close to our booth when they could.

It seemed no matter where we served God, He provided an opportunity for us to mingle with the public and love on them in the name of Jesus. We witnessed to people who had no thoughts of attending a church; some hearts were drastically changed through a genuine casual friendship. It was never about the sales; it was the hungry, hurting hearts which needed mending.

A side benefit was the opportunity for two love birds (me and Preacher Man if you haven't caught on by now) to spend time together as God continued to expand their ministries in ways they could not have envisioned.

43 - ANSWERING GOD'S CALL

"And when you pray…do not be like them, for your Father knows what you need before you ask him." Matthew 6:8 (ESV)

Once again, God saw Russell was needed at a small church halfway across the United States. Looking back, we now know He was preparing us for what our family would be needing as well.

After preaching in view of a call at First Baptist Church of Fair Play, Russell called me in California. "Susie, you will like Fair Play. It's Missouri country with lots of trees and flowers, chickens, cows, and a small convenience store on the highway for shopping. We can walk to church from the nice parsonage across the road. The best thing for you is, there is a little shed for your crafts and a flea market at the Sale Barn every week." I could tell by the excitement in his voice, this was not up for discussion. He knew it was God's call.

Our letter to our beloved First Baptist Church, Rohnert Park, California, sums it up best.

***

"Well, it's 69 degrees here in California as we write this letter; nice breeze, bright sunshine, and perfect day for a drive to the mountains or beach. In contrast, I'm told it was minus one (MINUS ONE DEGREE) in Southwest Missouri last night!

It seems we are called to give up a few things from time to time...

...roses growing all year round;

...balmy summer days and cool nights;

...fresh fruit all year round;

...walks along the beach;

...day trips to snowy mountains;

...watching God work miracles in young lives as He draws them to Himself.

Ah, but we do get some things in return...

...chiggers, ticks, flies;

...sticky, humid summers;

...cold, icy, snowy winters;

...brisk, tornado-like winds;

...carport replacing 20x20 garage/craft shop;

...and the list goes on, and on, and on.

Now for the REST OF THE STORY. We also get...

...another field ready to reap the harvest as God provides;

...to live within two hours of three of our children;

...AND OUR FIVE GRANDCHILDREN!

…and less than a two-hour drive for Susie to visit her Mother.

We have so missed our family the past ten years as we have served God in California. The ministry here has been both challenging and fruitful. The bonds God has created here are set for eternity; we treasure each one and will miss you terribly.

While thoughts of retirement crossed our minds, God had other plans. Surely by the time we move to our new location, God will warm the weather and prepare our hearts. We know He has prepared the one He has to lead this great church as you remain faithful.

Please continue to pray for us as we pray fervently for God to supply your needs. And, remember, our door is always open.

Because of souls, Brother Russell and Susie"

44 - FAMILY REUNITED

"Return to your home and declare how much God has done for you."
Luke 8:39 (ESV)

March 1994

With mixed feelings of sadness over leaving those we had grown close to and great anticipation of what was ahead, we were on our way once again in answer to God's call. We knew God was opening doors for us; golden opportunities to grow and serve. And a time to love on our family again.

Rural Fair Play in Polk County reminded us of our hometowns of Clarence and Goodman. On the traditional "Welcome Our New Pastor" Sunday, our family showed up in full force, practically outnumbering the congregation. We were home at last!

Mother was anxious to make the two-hour drive from her home in Webb City to spend a few days with us. She lived by herself and was very active in her church and community. We thought she was doing very well.

A few days after she arrived, she suddenly began hemorrhaging. We immediately took her to the emergency room where she was admitted to the hospital. She suffered with congestive heart failure, and her overall health was not as good as she had led us to believe.

At one point she seemed to have lost the will to survive; the doctors said prepare for the worst. This was not the homecoming we planned. For several weeks, I spent most of my time at the hospital with my precious mother. I begged God to please let her live; I asked forgiveness for the many times I casually said I could never take care of my head-strong mother. How I wanted more time with her.

For hours at a time in Citizen's Memorial Hospital, Bolivar, I held her hand, stroked her sweet face, sang gospel songs to her, and prayed my heart out. And, after seven long weeks, we got to bring Mother home to live with us. For several years she was ambulatory, and we did indeed spend many days doing crafts, shopping, and touring our beautiful Ozarks.

It was truly heaven on earth with Mother now living with us and our children and their families visiting often. With additional help in caring for Mother, we remained active in state pastor and wife retreats, evangelism conferences, and conventions.

Russell reading the Bible to Mother

On more than one occasion, Russell insisted he could take care of Mother so I could attend an overnight women's conference or girl's night out. She was able to fix her own meals and take care of herself during the day. However, neither of us were comfortable leaving her by herself overnight. When I returned, she bragged about his good care; even bringing her coffee and snacks. (Mother loved her son-in-law and I'm sure she was tickled to have his undivided attention.)

The church family welcomed Mother as they did us and made our first year there quite memorable. When the front steps became difficult for Mother, they immediately added a ramp. On

the days Mother couldn't make it to church, she could sit in her comfortable chair and watch the parking lot fill across the street. Several of the women dropped by periodically to visit with her. She was on the edge of her chair when the youth and children came to sing to her. God knew Mother needed to be ministered to by a loving church family in her final years.

During Mother's stay in the hospital, I heard a definite call from God to write a book about our story. He clearly had called me to write in high school, but I ignored the call. This was a difficult journey for me; I wasn't sure I could document my feelings. Truthfully, I'm not sure I wanted to let everyone know about our personal lives.

For a picture of God's grace, read my book, <u>My Mother My Child</u>, complete with helps for those caring for a loved one, whatever their age.

45 - FAIR PLAY MINISTRY

"And let us not be weary in well doing: for in due season we shall reap, if we faint not." Galatians 6:9 (KJV)

Meanwhile, back at Fair Play we were beginning a new chapter in our lives. As was his routine in every church, Russell immediately began visiting every home on the church roll in addition to his customary neighborhood walks and visits. Music Director, Bill Shook, his wife Shirley, and their family became close friends as we served together. It's heartwarming for me to watch the services online now and occasionally see their daughter, Paula, at the piano. Though Bill, Shirley, Russell, and countless other loved ones are awaiting us in Heaven, I feel sure God is continuing to answer their faithful prayers.

At Fair Play, I not only got to do Women's Ministries, but I also taught a Youth Sunday School class. We painted a big tree covering one wall in our classroom which we dubbed "The Blessing Tree". Each youth added their name to the tree as well as the names of friends needing prayer. In the summer, granddaughter Melissa helped me with children in Vacation Bible School. Another bonus of being home!

Sunday after Sunday, the altar filled with people praying for one another, accepting Jesus as their Savior, and yielding their lives to God's service. One seeking God's direction in his life was David (Leidra) Stunkel. David obeyed as God touched his heart and is currently pastor of Fair Play First Baptist Church. His children who were then in my Sunday School class are now married with families. What indescribable joy to experience God at work in the lives of His children.

Attending state conventions and conferences such as Windermere Bible Conference gave Russell opportunity to renew old acquaintances from prior Missouri pastorates. He also met ministers from neighboring associations such as Roger and Ruth Easter from Louisburg First Baptist Church in Dallas County. Long before we knew what the future held for us, God was building friendships, which continue to this day.

Joe Coppedge and Russell

When the Polk County Association needed a Director of Missions (DOM), Russell invited a pastor friend from Oklahoma, Joe Coppedge, to use his pulpit to preach in view of a call. A life-long friend of Russell, former pastor and a former Director of Missions, Otis Divine, tried his best to get Russell to submit his name but he was quick to respond. "Otis, God has called me to pastor. I have no interest in anything else. I've worked with the Directors of Missions in every church field I have served. Their job is important and challenging, but not for me."

Joe Coppedge accepted the position and he and his wife, Judy, did a superb job ministering to the Polk County churches until God called Joe home in 2019.

One of the more fun activities the two of us organized was a dinner for our deacons and their wives. Believe it or not, we planned and prepared the entire meal. Together we decorated the tables and welcomed our guests.

As an after-dinner activity, each deacon was given a sack full of "stuff" with instructions to create an Easter bonnet for his wife which she would then have to wear. Two miracles not to miss: Amazing even us, (1) we did it all ourselves, and (2) they let Russell continue as their pastor!

Close to my heart in Missouri was Baptist Children's Home Ministry and their annual quilt auction to raise funds. Every year we tried to set aside at least $500 for me to bid on quilts; it was addictive! If bidding was stuck at $100, I upped the bid, usually dropping out at two or three hundred dollars. It didn't always work out; I have a few quilts I never intended to purchase. My favorite "intentional" purchase was the quilt I helped the Fair Play ladies make; I treasure it today. (Thank you, June, for making me learn to quilt in California! Only God knew where that would lead!)

My growing stack of quilts enabled us to begin a family tradition. When a grandchild or great grandchild turned thirteen, they could choose a handmade quilt. At sixteen, there was a trip to the Christian Bookstore for them to pick out a Bible and have their name engraved on the cover.

Russell was in his seventies when he felt it was time to retire. Desiring to stay close to Mother's doctors, we searched for rentals within a few miles of Bolivar. These proved to be too expensive and not adequate for our needs. When we turned our search to a fixer-upper with little down, we nearly gave up. Most of the fixer-uppers, in our opinion, needed a match struck to them.

Joe & Judy Coppedge

Youth serenades Mother
Deacons Made Hats for their Wives

FBC Fair Play MO.

Fair Play First Baptist provided us a beautiful, well-kept parsonage. When we left, the church generously used the parsonage for missionaries on furlough. David Stunkel followed Russell as pastor, and he owned his home in Fair Play.

God always more than supplied our needs. It was up to us to keep praying and searching for the home we knew He had in store for us. We continued to trust our miracle-working Father as we reluctantly expanded our search to adjoining Dallas County.

46 - WHERE THE BUFFALO ROAM

"By wisdom, a house is built, and through understanding, it is established; through knowledge its rooms are filled with rare and beautiful treasures."
Proverbs 24:3-4 (NIV)

December 1999

Buffalo, Missouri, the county seat of Dallas County; a rural community about thirty miles east of Fair Play and 30 miles north of Springfield, Missouri.

When we arrived at the Realtor's Office, we were met by agent Aaron Taylor who was prepared to show us "The Doll House". Although this listing had few of our specific needs such as three bedrooms, Aaron insisted we see this property before checking out any other listings.

On a very cold, blustery November day, we pulled into the driveway of a tiny house on a bumpy gravel road. Immediately when I saw all the trees, I began to cry. Aaron continued to show Russell the house while I tried to get myself together. Suddenly, the size of the house didn't matter; I kept thinking, would God really let me have all those trees? When I finally made it to the back porch, a squirrel was perched on a limb fussing at me as if to say, "this is my tree, and you can't have it!" I fussed back!

Before we committed to buying any property, we had agreed that we should look it over individually as if we were going to live there by ourselves. Hopefully, this was the last move for either of us; it needed to meet our individual needs. As we proceeded to purchase the property, we came to realize a bank, grocery store, Dollar General store, and a family restaurant were only a mile and a half back down the road. We joked that when we could no longer drive on the highway, we could still take care of our own needs.

There was to be no more looking at houses; we immediately agreed that we had found our dream home. In a short time, the paperwork was completed, and we were planning our move.

Although we closed on Adams' Acre January 5, 2000, Russell did not resign Fair Play First Baptist until the end of March. This gave us three months to prepare for retirement. There were enough furnishings in our new home for us to spend the night when we could. We had a neighbor who occasionally stayed with Mother when we needed to be away overnight. This made it possible for us to spend several nights in our new home before anyone knew we were moving.

Our patience was tested on our first overnight stay as we assembled a computer desk. After a few prayer-filled hours, the project was miraculously completed. It was worth the effort as we stretched our weary bones out on the bed and took in the scenery out our big window. A winter wonderland unfolded before our eyes as a blanket of heavy snow covered the ground and clung to the chain link fence. Red birds, bluebirds, and squirrels were at play in our back yard. We were like newlyweds again as we snuggled together knowing everything was going to be okay. God was showering His unconditional love on our family in retirement beyond our wildest expectations.

As usual, God was providing more than we could have hoped for. We did not have extra funds to repair an old house. The "Doll House" was completely remodeled, from kitchen cabinetry to painting and decorating. Floor-to-ceiling bookshelves lining one wall in the master bedroom were perfect for a pastor's books. The second bedroom doors were wide enough to accommodate Mother's wheelchair. The extra-adjoining bathroom featured a nice shower, and a walk-in closet. The home seemed ready-made for Mother down to the convenient no-step entry through the garage. A nice daybed in the extra-long living room could serve as the third bedroom.

Our Heavenly Father gave my nature-loving mother two big porches where she could enjoy the changing seasons and wildlife. In winter, she could watch the birds and squirrels play in the snow while warming her toes by the fireplace. Springtime was sure to please with wildflowers, dogwood, and redbud trees in the front yard.

As a side note, Aaron Taylor became more than the agent who sold us our dream home. The day he showed us 'The Doll House', he was nervously watching his phone for a call from his wife, Angie. She was expecting their second child and had gestational diabetes which meant getting an ultrasound at the hospital every other day to make sure the baby was alive. Beautiful little Ryann Shea was born January 21. Her five-year-old brother, Nathan's birthday was June 15.

Angie's Dad, Kenny McDaniel, was active in the Dallas County Association and was pleased when Aaron told him about the retired preacher moving into town. A seed was planted. A bonus joy: we later witnessed Aaron surrender his life to the gospel ministry, participated in his ordination and continued to watch their family grow as he became pastor of nearby Windyville Baptist Church.

Adams' Acres was and is the perfect home. It was perfect for the three of us for four years and for the two of us for over sixteen years. Now alone, there is no place I have lived coast to coast that compares to the peace, joy, and comfort I have here on Adams' Acres. My loving Father knows the beginning and the end; His plan is always right. His ways are perfect.

As wonderful as retirement and finding the perfect home was, God had only begun to surprise us. Preacher Man would soon have a major decision to make; one only God could orchestrate.

Ricky's happy with Cousin Penny's Painting

HELP, Susie!

The Christmas Story

Family ~ the Best Gift of All

GREAT GRANDS

Ivy and Aubrey

Granny Sue with great grands

Daisy. TJ, and Lexy

47 - COUNTRY LIVING AT ITS BEST

"Trust the Lord with all your heart, and lean not unto your own understanding. In all your ways acknowledge Him and He will give you the desires of your heart." Proverbs 3:5-6 (KJV)

Russell began his daily walk on our long gravel road even before we had completely moved in. A small Mennonite community was around the bend and, of course, he wasted no time getting acquainted. Jess and Nancy Hostetler owned the home nearest ours. We not only watched their little children grow up and have families of their own, but we also became good friends with Jess's parents as well. His father, Elmer, stopped by periodically to discuss the Bible with Russell. Quite often he brought me a fresh loaf of his wife's homemade bread!

We got acquainted with our next-door neighbors, Doug and Betsy Earls and their daughter, Anna, right away. Doug pastored Calvary Freewill Baptist and invited Russell to preach for him a

Russell, Anna Earls, and Susie

The Rebel and Preacher Man

few times. Betsy and Anna stopped by to visit Mother often with little gifts and hugs. Mother loved the attention.

Our first order of business after knowing where we were going to live was to find a new church home. This was a new journey for us since Russell was not pastoring a church. Aaron was quick to invite us to his church and Mrs. Ina Chapman, of the local furniture store, all but insisted we visit her church right away. We visited both and several others as we continued to seek God's direction. It was Jess Hostetler who told Russell about a new church building going up five miles south of town.

The membership of Church Grove Baptist was building a new facility along busy 65 Highway. This was another of God's appointments as we joined the congregation in time to help on the building and become charter members. Pastor Ron Lilley and the congregation named the new facility Crossroads Baptist Church. Our grandson Rusty visited before the flooring was installed and, along with us,

Rusty

wrote his favorite scripture on the foundation in the sanctuary. Pastor Ron Lilley, his wife, Pauline and children, Rick, Rhonda, and Lajeana quickly became lifetime friends as we worked together to reach our communities.

After our move, we held an open house in May. Friends from Springfield, Joplin, Fair Play, and the Southern Baptist College in Bolivar rejoiced with us at what the Lord had done. Our children and grandchildren were pleased we were going to stay in Missouri.

ICE STORM 2007

The skunk survived the horrific ice storm of 2007, but he didn't make it past Preacher Man!

From day one, I coveted the five acres adjoining our "Adams' Acre" (one, long skinny acre). Those five acres were for sale when we moved in, but the price was more than we could afford at the time. Our entire family knew I had labeled the property "God's Five" as I diligently prayed God would one day make a way for it to be "Our Five." A year passed and young Jeff and Amber Abercrombie bought "God's Five" and began clearing their land. I took pictures with mixed emotions. However, their family began to grow, and they put the property up for sale again.

The Rebel and Preacher Man

This time we were able to buy it. I had saved an extra "S" for the mailbox which now reads "Adams Acres!" I continued to thank God daily for His generosity to us while I thanked Him for providing a better piece of property for the Abercrombie family.

Meanwhile, we continued to work on our home and property. In season I picked wild blackberries, elderberries, and gooseberries from the fence rows. The first two years we filled our truck bed with black walnuts from the walnut grove in the valley. There were lamb's quarters, poke, dandelion, and other greens for the taking.

In addition to all the edibles on our property, there was an abundance of four-leaf clovers to be found. To understand my husband's patience, you had to have watched him sit on the mower at the top of the hill while I searched through a patch of clover in the valley below. I have a four-leaf clover pressed in most every book I own, for what reason, I don't know!

Our first year, Pastor Lyle Mankey and a team from Macks Creek First Baptist Church spent a Saturday clearing our fence rows and burning brush. Years later, after we purchased "God's Five", Olive Point Southern Baptist worked all day helping clear more of our land. Pastor Terry Gentry, Jr. remembers it well; … something about poison ivy, I think.

Preparing for the possibility of a long-term interim, Russell enrolled in the Center for Congregational Health in Springfield and successfully completed classes to qualify to serve as Interim Pastor whenever and wherever needed. It was

exciting times for us as we visited the Dallas County Southern Baptist Association's churches. He introduced himself to the pastors and gave them his resume for supply or interim.

It was exciting to visit different churches and meet their pastors and leadership, but we were equally pleased to worship in our home church. However, less than three months after we settled in, our lives again took a turn. During our first summer in Dallas County, a search committee was formed to find a new Director of Missions. Russell was quick to assure them of his prayers as they began the search. He was content doing supply and interim work and reassured me he had no interest whatsoever in becoming a Director of Missions.

Our family in prayer

We had really missed our children while in California. Our move to Missouri meant seeing them more often. However, while he pastored, time was limited. Now, being retired we were ready for family gatherings. Debbie, Ricky, and Michael each lived within two hours of Buffalo so they could gather often on Adams Acres.

Laura and me in LA

Happy Momma

Although Laura had piano students and other work in California, this was a bright spot for me. Travel! How fun to hop a plane and spend a week with my girl.

48 - PREACHER MAN ON THE LOOSE

"You are my strength, I watch for you; you, God, are my fortress."
Psalm 59:9 (KJV)

Russell's love for God, for life, and for people seemed to spill out all around him in whatever he did and wherever he went. Now, retired and still full of energy, he was like a child in a candy store. I don't think he ever concerned himself with what others thought of him or his actions. His typical visit to the Post Office explains it best.

"How much do you owe me for mailing my letters at this Post Office?" He seems dead serious as he hands an envelope and a couple small boxes to the postal clerk. It doesn't matter to him if there is a line of people waiting to mail packages; he acts as though he is the only patron. Of course, he quickly pulls out his billfold as he waits for the heavy items to be weighed.

In another store he may ask, "What do you have for free today? I'm kinda low on money." A few minutes of casual, crazy conversation opens a friendship and trust enabling him to be there for those clerks when they have problems or questions. His main goal was to share Jesus.

He had a ready answer for anyone who asked his name. "My name is Adams, Russell Adams, I'm kin to Adam and Eve. Do you know about them?"

One summer, he stopped at a construction tent set up on the grocery store parking lot to chat. Day after day, he poked his head in and built up a relationship with the workers. He rushed home one day to tell me one of those workers asked Jesus to forgive his sins and come into his heart. It was Preacher Man's motivation, his bottom line, his reason for being.

Max Davolt, AG Pastor Shaulis, and Russell

Russell walked every day for his health and for enjoyment. When we were in Fair Play, he walked at the Southern Baptist College field house in Bolivar. I wish I had written down all the stories he told me about people he met on his walks. He had opportunities to pray with many; others he simply enjoyed getting acquainted with them.

No matter where we shopped, whether grocery store or Walmart, most of the clerks (and customers) not only knew Russell; they also knew he was going to talk about Jesus at every opportunity.

Speaking of shopping, I'll give you another glimpse of his patience. Neither of us were big shoppers. However, seasonal markdowns were the exception, especially between Christmas and New Year. Beginning when our kids were in school, I kept a dresser drawer filled with "treasures" to give to people who serve us; or are lonely; or need Jesus. The kids were free to shop in the treasure drawer when they needed a gift. So, when Dollar General, Walmart, or another chain was marking down items I could use in my goody drawer, I mapped out a route of all their stores from Buffalo to Springfield. Beginning early in the day, we hit each one. Russell waited in the car while I shopped. We made sure there was one store with room for his walk. Then a hearty lunch and back to shopping.

Joy in the Journey

Paul & Joyce Dunlap

Aleene Love

Bob & Sue Lyon

Jody Johnston

Cliff and Eunice Long

RUSSELL'S DAILY WALKS

provided the opportunity to
*make new friends
*build relationships
*share Jesus's love
and
*pray for and encourage

49 - YIELDING TO GOD'S ULTIMATE PLAN

"Whether you turn to the right or to the left, your ears will hear a voice behind you, saying, 'this is the way; walk in it.'"
Isaiah 30:21 (NIV)

July 2000

You have figured out I am the rebel in this story, right? Have you noticed Preacher Man had a bit of rebel spirit in him as well? He had absolutely no intentions of ever becoming anything more than a country preacher caring for his flock. To him, it was a high honor, not to be taken lightly. Now retired, he planned to encourage other churches and pastors by helping in the pulpit where needed; staying faithful to the association's programs and continuing to tell all in his path about his Jesus.

Remember those "chance meetings" we had with the Easters? It was Roger Easter, Interim Director of Missions of Dallas County, who approached Russell about the position. When Otis Divine heard of the search for DOM in Dallas County Association, he immediately suggested Russell apply for the position. After long discussions and much prayer, he hesitantly submitted his resume to the Search Committee for consideration.

"Don't worry, Susie. They aren't going to call a 74-year-old, worn-out preacher to lead this fine association. If they do invite me to preach in view of a call, I can tell you, it will have to be a strong vote for me to accept. I don't think you have anything to worry about." He confidently told Otis he would commit to serving three years if by some miracle they actually called him.

In July 2000, with a 100% vote, a reluctant preacher ended his half-year retirement and began a journey as Director of Missions of Dallas County Southern Baptist Association. At the end of three years, he accepted Otis' challenge to serve another five. Before those five years had passed, God called Otis Divine Home.

And two surprised senior adults began another phase of learning, adjusting, relinquishing our wills to the Father's will as God began to direct our paths.

We immediately set up an office in our home and I became his Ministry Assistant. This was perfect for us since Mother's health continued to fail. My job was to keep an up-to-date church list, a current membership roll from each church, and to mail out a monthly newsletter and other state and local promotions. Thank you, northern California and Steve and Sherri White, for the computer and training! As always, God provided for our future needs.

The DOM was to work two days a week and to visit churches on Sunday, supplying the pulpit when needed. We originally planned for Tuesday to be the day we were available in our home office. That plan lasted about two weeks; we were obviously not accustomed to the rural, farmland setting of our county. When folks came into town, whatever day it happened to be, they wanted to take care of all their business. So, we quickly wrote in the newsletter, "If we are home, the office is open".

It was a blessing in disguise to have the office in our home as it met Mother's needs as well as our own. She was treated by all like Queen of the Castle. I'm forever grateful to those who spent a few minutes with her when they came to our home for Committee Meetings. Several like Thelbert Gott of Union Mound dropped by while in town to watch the birds with Mother; it blessed my heart. She never got to attend our churches, but she did get to know and love many of the people. This could only

The Rebel and Preacher Man

happen in small town USA, and only by God's direction.

If you are thinking this sounds like a pretty casual job situation, hold on. Only God knew our entire relaxed country lifestyle was about to make a drastic change.

Otis and Russell

Two of God's "Little Boys" each with a burning passion to make Jesus known.

The Divine and Adams families had worked and played together since the seventies. Soon after we married, Otis and Judy were called to a neighboring church field and we continued that relationship through forty years. At this writing, the three are them are with their beloved Savior.

Jeff Metcalf, Ft. Madison, Iowa, found us on Facebook. He was anxious to find his former pastor from FBC Ewing, MO. Russell had a profound influence on Jeff as a teen and he wanted to tell him so. He spent several days with us; later we stayed with him and his family in Iowa.

Russell, Jill Hostetler, Jeff Metcalf at the Buffalo Victorian Steakhouse

God's family knows no bounds.

50 - WHAT HAPPENED TO OUR CALENDAR?

"Oh, continue Your lovingkindness to those who know You, and Your righteousness to the upright in heart." Psalm 36:10 (NKJV)

A bit of clarity here for my readers who may not be familiar with the Southern Baptist denomination and "calling" a Director of Missions. For Southern Baptists, the state convention is broken down into regions. Each region is led by an ordained minister called Director of Missions and other officers as it chooses. The Director will have the responsibility of working with individual churches and pastors as the Lord directs. He is "called" by the association and voted on by its leaders. The Director of Missions is responsible for encouraging, providing training, and overseeing the group and individuals as needed.

***

Dallas County Association of Southern Baptists'(DCASB) quarterly Executive Board meetings are held in February, May, August, and November. Thankfully, we attended the February and May executive board meetings and were familiar with the leadership and ministries.

The following excerpts taken from the 2000 Annual of the Dallas County Association of Southern Baptists will provide a glimpse of how God re-arranged our schedules.

To consider calling Russell Adams as their Director of Missions, the association called for a Special Meeting of Executive Board, Thursday, July 6, 2000, Buffalo First Baptist Church.

The Rebel and Preacher Man

Moderator Roger Easter opened in prayer. Clerk Alecia Holman called the roll: every church present plus visitors. Music Director, Ruth Easter led music. Denzil Webb, DOM Search Committee Chair, made the introduction and presentation of Bro. Russell A. Adams. (DOM Search Committee: Denzil Webb, Herb Mallard, and Curtis Adams)

Bro. Adams led the members in prayer and preached from 1 Thessalonians 1:5-10. He pointed out this scripture revealed the strengths and weaknesses of the model church which was a powerful example of belief in the Holy Spirit, evangelistic in spirit, and energetic in service. Bro. Adams said this is the vision he has for DCASB. He closed with an invitation and prayer.

During a question-and-answer time, Brother Adams expressed his desire to do new, interesting, energizing, and evangelistic things in the association. Currently participating in the Interim Pastor Intentional Program, he stressed the importance of continued training for all Christians. Although he has never been a DOM, he stated he has served almost every position in an association. He has a desire to be pastor to pastors, and supply the pulpit as needed. Susie will do the office work including composing and mailing a monthly newsletter to the members of every church.

Russell and Susie were excused while other questions or discussions were presented and a vote by ballot was taken. Mark Still, Ben Thatcher, and Terry Gentry, Sr. tallied the votes; a unanimous vote of YES to call Bro. Russell Adams as DOM; part time, working two days a week and available on Sunday to visit or supply.

***

Russell would be called to preside over the next quarterly Executive Board Meeting in six weeks. His first DCASB Annual Meeting was in September, less than three months away. (We pulled off a wedding in one month; this should be a snap!) And so it was, because of overwhelming support from committees and pastors.

***

111th Annual Meeting September 14, 2000, Union Mound Southern Baptist Church, Elkland, Missouri

The host church, Union Mound Southern Baptist Church in Elkland is a small church with a big spirit. Located seventeen miles south of Buffalo, it was a beautiful drive ablaze with fall colors, deer, and turkey; the church building, grounds, and adjoining cemetery were in pristine shape as they welcomed a record crowd.

Excerpts from meeting:

"Association approved two items presented by DOM Russell: open the 2001 annual meeting with an evangelistic service on Monday; adopt 'Laborers Together with God' as a theme for the association.

Martha Spicer, MBC Stewardship Consultant, gave the Baptist Foundation Report. (Read my thoughts about Martha in chapter 32. I believe my Father in Heaven has a sense of humor.)

Pastor Dinzel Webb presented "Broken and Spilled Out" as special music. Pastor Terry Gentry, Sr. and his wife, Beverly, presented the Obituary Service and led in singing "Precious Memories". (Only God knew in 21 years, Terry, Sr., would be called as DCASB Director of Missions.)

The following pastors are scheduled to preach the DCASB

Revival September 17-22 at the Shewmaker Center, Buffalo: Sunday, Mark Still, Harmony; Monday, Kenneth Mizer, Plad; Tuesday, Ben Thatcher, Windyville; Wednesday, Russell Adams, DOM; Thursday, Terry Gentry, Jr., Olive Point; Friday, Terry Gentry, Sr., Pisgah."

51 - SEEKING GOD'S DIRECTION IN MINISTRY

"Seek the LORD and His strength; Seek His face evermore!"
1 Chronicles 16:11 (NKJV)

Once we got past the busyness of the scheduled fall meetings, Russell began to pray seeking God's direction. From the beginning, he carried a burden for pastors and their families. We knew firsthand the challenges facing pastors and their need for support. He sought ways to bring them together, to encourage them, and to provide opportunities for growth as he held each up in prayer.

One of our preferred places for regular pastor and wife outings was Buffalo's Victorian Steakhouse. After sharing a meal together, men and women could move to separate rooms for a time of sharing and prayer. We knew firsthand the value of building relationships among pastors and their families. Having a safe place to share blessings and concerns was a priority in his ministry for all ages.

Russell had a deep appreciation for those God called to shepherd His flock. He spent much time in prayer for every pastor and for his ministry. Through the years, he felt blessed by God to work with young men who felt called into ministry. I have heard him tell of the challenges accompanying a call of God on your life. He counseled many new preacher boys and their wives and felt honored to work with them one on one.

My heart immediately turned to the women and girls in our smaller congregations. Already meeting regularly for Bible studies and fellowships, Crossroads ladies were inspired to help plan events for the association. With God's help and cooperation from the churches, the first annual Dallas County Association

Ladies' Retreat was held in the new Crossroads Baptist Church in the Spring of 2001. The annual retreat continues to this day and has expanded to other women's ministries with a new director and younger women climbing on board.

Spencer Hutson, Terry Gentry, Jr., Steve Simko, Dr. Yeats, and Russell

At our age, we were aware of the need to minister to our oft forgotten senior adults. In California, we had participated in a ministry called Kaleb's Kids. Senior adults from various denominations gathered at Mt. Gilead Bible Camp each month for a fun, inspirational program, lunch, and hands-on mission opportunities. Kaleb's Kids was named after Caleb who, at eighty-five-years old, claimed his mountain. (Read Numbers chapters thirteen and fourteen.) DCASB's Kaleb's Kids grew quickly.

Dr. Yeats and Director of Missions, Russell Adams, pray across Missouri

Since our churches each took a turn hosting, Kaleb's Kids also gave senior adults the opportunity to visit sister churches and learn how to pray for them. Participants were asked to bring poems, stories, or music; the host pastor provided a message. Contributory lunch and fellowship followed. Herb Mallard was first to quote a scripture passage, followed by Albert Kerns with a story. Engaging our senior adults to share their talents, prayers, and concerns strengthened our churches. The summer months were fun because many brought kids, who were out of school, to share in the program.

Christmas meant a banquet at a local restaurant with guest preachers and musicians and presents for everyone. Summer months meant Family BBQ at nearby Bennett Spring State Park.

When a DCASB Stewardship Rally presented seven individuals from youth to senior adults who gave testimonies of God's blessing their faithfulness in giving, new DOM Russell had a ready reply: "This should be done annually in each church. Teaching people to give God their first fruits would change our world."

Susie with Missouri Baptist Convention Director of Missions wives and Sharon Yeats

The Rebel and Preacher Man

The Three Rascals —
Roger
Ronald
Russell

Ketsup → DOM Russell in charge!

Ladies' Retreat — Honoring Pastors' Wives

Preachers — and they say women talk...

Each year we saw new ministries; mission trips, brotherhood workdays, sing-a-longs, and more in DCASB. In addition, we continued to attend every state and regional event we could: pastor and wife retreats, Bible studies and conferences. We learned firsthand: God's children are never too old to grow.

52 - INSPIRING TIMES OF REFRESHING

"...For your Father knows the things you have need of before you ask Him."
Matthew 6:8b (KJV)

I endeavor to move my pen as God directs while the familiar sound of old hymns refreshes my heart and soul. The peace of Christ fills the room as Ruth Marshall's beautiful piano CD plays non-stop.

The CD was a gift, one of many, given to us by Dr. John Marshall and the Second Baptist Church of Springfield, Missouri. Early in our new journey as Director of Missions, we received an invitation to dinner hosted by Second Baptist Church. Dr. Marshall and his team planned a season of time to encourage, pray for, and pamper the Directors of Missions and their families in our region of the state.

A bit about Dr. John Marshall: Dr. John Marshall pastored Second Baptist Church in Springfield from 1995-2019. After serving as Second Vice-President and First Vice-President of the Missouri Baptist Convention, he was elected President in 2010.

> To learn more about Dr. Marshall and read his inspiring blogs, go to
> www.john316marshall.com

Even as he faced serious health issues of his own, he was ready and able to encourage others in ministry. His letter to our region's Directors of Missions says it best.

Dear Southwest Missouri Directors of Missions,

My poor health, two heart attacks and a stroke since October, has slowed my work, including our follow-up ministry to you. I'm sorry for the delay. Thanks for your prayers on my behalf. Please keep interceding for me. I am living on the prayers of God's people.

Enclosed is the gift we long ago promised. I hope you will enjoy it. We want to bless you and your wife.

I remind you we want to honor you and your wife on Sunday night, May 16. Be sure you keep that night free on your calendar. Our goal is to treat you like royalty that night.

It is an honor to be your co-laborer. I love you. God bless you in all ways always.

Grace,
Bro. John 3:16

The gift, one of many, was a season pass to Silver Dollar City. It came at a time when we were personally not able to splurge on such an event. This generous and timely gift enabled us to have someone stay with Mother a few days and have a respite.

Another gift, notably the most valuable one, from Dr. Marshall and his church, was the promise to pray for us. Each Director of Missions was adopted by one of Second Baptist's Sunday School classes. They held us up in daily prayer and sent encouraging cards throughout the year. Only heaven will reveal the impact of their faithful prayers for one reluctant DOM and his

The Rebel and Preacher Man

family as well as on so many others.

Most likely it was this gift of constant prayer for us that prompted Russell to initiate a program in our association for individuals to pray for a different church each week. Our association continues the process to this day as we reap the fruit of our labors.

Dr. John and Ruth Marshall are one of the most humble, loving couples we ever met. Their main mission is to share Jesus 24/7. When I wrote my first book, *My Mother My Child*, it was John and Ruth who held our family up in prayer from day one. He quickly added it to his church's library. No matter where he was or who he was with, he applauded my writings and encouraged us in our ministries. He became an inspiration to us to do the same for others.

There is a love God imparts in the hearts of those who truly believe and follow Him that radiates into the world around them. I believe Preacher Man's life expressed that kind of love wherever he went.

Find Dr. John Marshall's website
For inspiration and encouragement!

http://www.john316marshall.com/

53 - A NEW MOUNTAIN TO CLIMB

"Behold, I will do a new thing, Now it shall spring forth; Shall you not know it? I will even make a road in the wilderness And rivers in the desert."
Isaiah 43:19 (KJV)

From the first day I entered Harmony Heights Baptist Church and met their bold preacher, God has been training this rebel. Perhaps my next book should be titled: "The First Time I...". What a mountain- conquering journey; I trust you can tell it continues to be an amazing journey with no end in sight.

It was a sad day when Center Point Baptist voted to close its doors and turn everything over to our association. In due time, Crossroads Baptist voted to consider a restart and Pastor Ron Lilley began forming teams for an in-person survey of the area.

Ken McCune, Church Planting Strategist with our Missouri Baptist Convention, was invited to help us survey the area in preparation for a restart. Russell and I went out to survey with Helen Wall as our driver.

"I'll get this one," Russell said. "It's been a long, hot day. You girls keep the car cool and pray while I do this one." Only God knew why he needed to go alone to this home.

The door opened slightly and a young man wearing a cap casually visited with Russell through the screen door. They talked, and talked, and talked. About the time Helen was reaching to turn the car off for a while, the young man removed his cap as he stepped out onto his porch. "Don't touch the key, Helen. Don't move! Pray!"

As we prayed our hearts out, Russell led a young father, Victor Williams, to faith in Jesus as his Savior and Lord. We wept and prayed as we watched them shake hands and hug. Russell was beaming. The angels were rejoicing. (Luke 15:10) God was honored; and we were spell-bound!

Clearly God wanted a church in that neighborhood. The old church was located on Center Point Road, hence the name Center Point Baptist. The entire committee felt we should keep part of the original name; hence, Promise Point Baptist Church was born.

Vacation Bible School at Promise Point

We were two of seventeen adults from the founding church who became charter members of the newly formed Promise Point Baptist Church. One of our first families from the neighborhood to join Promise Point was the Victor Williams family. Russell also led Victor's wife, Michelle, to Jesus as she sat in her car in front of the church. What a joy to see this young family in Sunday School and worship on Sunday.

Brother Ken McCune, his wife Shyre, and son Brent were with us for several months as the church took hold and began to grow. As memory serves me, Shyre's father was interim pastor for a while, followed by Daryl Patterson, and Clifton Long. The church has undergone a few changes including location but continues to thrive.

It was a time to affirm what I believed and why I believed it as we focused on doctrines and writing and adopting a constitution. We determined which officers and committees were needed, how to structure the Sunday School and worship services, and so much more. I gained a new appreciation for those pioneers who began our churches with prayer, God's vision, and perseverance. It continues to break my heart as I watch congregations slowly drift

Neighborhood visitors

away and another dream collapse.

May God forgive me for the times on our trips I casually remarked, "You could be pastor of that little church over there." What an honor to serve the small church with precious saints who have weathered the storm of life and come out bolder and stronger in their faith. I've learned to pray for every church we pass, whatever the denomination, that they proclaim Jesus is Lord and the Father glorified.

54 - SPEAKING OF MOUNTAINS

"Before the mountains were created, before the earth was formed, you are God without beginning or end." Psalm 90:2 (KJV)

Many of my best childhood memories center around summer camps. I am convinced the influence of faithful teachers in camps and Bible schools prepared me for my unbelievable future as a pastor's wife. We looked forward to praying for and supporting each church's Vacation Bible School.

When summer camps were held near Macks Creek, the Association prepared all the food. Alecia Holman, the cook, planned the menu and stocked the kitchen. Each church was assigned a day or two to send a team to help prepare the meals, serve, and clean up.

They eventually switched to Eagle Rock Retreat Center in the Mark Twain National Forest. It's a beautiful camp with exceptional facilities for the kids. And... the center furnished all the meals! Camp Directors could hire charter buses or use church vans to transport the kids, staff, and equipment.

We eagerly made it a practice to attend the first day of camp. Leaving the house early, we enjoyed a good lunch on the way, and arrived an hour ahead of the kids. I can't even describe the excitement and joy it was for us as we stood outside the dorms and gathered hugs from these kiddos. God's Amazing Family at its best.

***

August 20, 2015

The trek into the campgrounds had been unusually slow; miles of unpaved roads were washed out by recent storms. We arrived safely, gathered hugs and joyful stories from "our kids," and enjoyed dinner as the sky darkened. Hoping to get out of the woods and onto paved roads before the storm hit, we left early.

As we left the lowlands and started up one of the hills, the storm hit. Lightning, thunder, and rain slowed us to a crawl. By now we were midway up a steep, narrow dirt road with no way to turn around. We could not see the road signs that would have directed us to the right path. There was no choice but to stay on the main road as high winds stirred the canopy of tree limbs above us. We had to stop periodically to remove small limbs that had fallen across the road.

We came to a complete stop just as we topped one of the steep hills. A downed tree was sprawled completely across the road in front of us. There was no turning back. There was no phone signal. Backing down the road was not an option. We were stuck! Or were we?

The tree must be moved. Seriously? Yes. "Our Father in Heaven – HELP YOUR CHILDREN!"

We devised a plan. Together we could pull the top of the tree back as far as we could. One could then try to hold it back while the other moved the vehicle forward. We both thought I should try to hold the tree while he quickly hopped into the car and moved it forward.

Together in the blinding rain, we grabbed hold of the stronger branches and tugged: And tugged and tugged and tugged. Finally, we thought we made a path wide enough to get the car through without driving too close to the muddy edge of the cliff. I held the end of the tree back as far as I could so he could turn loose and hop into the car. We figured he could move faster than I. Just as he hopped into the car, I felt the limbs breaking. Crack!

Crack! Crack! Plop! Just as he pulled forward, the tree smacked the trunk of the car.

Lightning continued to flash like a camera snapping pictures as I worked my way through the downed tree toward the waiting vehicle. As I reached up to open the door, my foot slipped, and down I went into the mud. Muddy! Gravel road! Pouring rain! Russell could not see what was happening outside the car. With God's help, I managed to get up and pull my muddy body into the car.

We knew we must keep going as long as we could see the road ahead. Soaked to the bone, muddy, and not a clue where we were heading, we were still happy campers. We had a peace only God can give. I am convinced we were safely held in our Father's hands by the prayers of an entire camp of young people!

We made it off the mountain with no more disasters. We were way off course, but the sun came out for a beautiful ride

My tree in winter

home. We obviously did not stop for coffee or anything else. However, you will not believe this: God knows it is true. We neared "my Tree" around sunset and, without saying a word, Preacher Man slowed our muddy vehicle down for me to snap a picture. I LOVE THAT MAN!

55 - SUSIE'S UNPLANNED FORTY DAY RESPITE

"My help comes from the Lord, the Maker of heaven and earth."
Psalms 121:2 (KJV)

Monday, September 28, 2015

"Honey, you need to take me to the Buffalo clinic. I can't seem to get rid of this congestion. Maybe they will order a prescription."

After a few tests, it was determined I had a collapsed lung. My oxygen was 73%. I was immediately taken by ambulance to Bolivar's Citizen's Memorial Hospital. I learned firsthand the feeling of being out of control. I had nothing but the clothes I left home in, and Russell had no idea where any of my things were at home. There was no time to prepare my spoiled hubby for a solo flight. Life froze in place for us that day.

When the hospital's routine procedures failed, there was talk of sending me to a Springfield hospital for surgery. I was more worried over Russell having to drive to Springfield than the possibility of surgery. As I pondered the situation, our pastor, Cliff Long "just happened" to come in. He immediately prayed, asking God to intervene, and God answered. I was not transferred and did not have surgery, although I was in for a prolonged stay beginning with the next seven days in ICU. I was sick; very, very sick.

Because I've had a life-long weight problem, I kept putting my emphasis on eating better, moving more, thinking I could improve how I felt. Earlier, a friend warned me something was wrong; I shrugged my shoulders. I was going to take care of myself! Hmm! Sounds a bit like a rebel to me.

God got my attention, I yielded to the situation in a new way as I began to thank Him for taking care of me when I was too stubborn to do it myself. I prayed for Him to give me opportunities to witness while there.

My amazing husband called me every morning, visited at least once a day, and called me again before I went to bed. Not having me at home for forty days was a real learning curve for him. I made the coffee; he would have to learn. I did all the laundry, so he went to see Hal at Chapman's Furniture to learn how to operate our washer and dryer.

Taking care of my clothes was certainly out of his domain. My friend, Helen Wall, came to the rescue; she helped him find my clothes and other things I needed. Judy Coppedge (Mrs. DOM Joe) immediately began checking my closet while in rehab and took clothing home to wash and iron for me.

Russell maintained a heavy schedule during my stay including an exciting week-long revival at Harmony Baptist Church at Phillipsburg. Pastor Keith and Penny Wingo picked him up each night, so he didn't have to drive. I'm sure they, and our other churches as well, prayed daily for my recovery and for Russell.

Over half of my forty-day respite was spent in Bolivar at the Parkview Healthcare Facility for therapy and rehab. Besides needing to regain strength in my entire body, I developed severe cellulitis in both legs. I was weak for quite a while and wheeled everywhere. I recall the first time I walked (very slowly) to the lunchroom. God was making sure I established an exercise routine to continue at home.

I was overwhelmed by the visits, calls, and cards I received. There is no way to acknowledge them all, but two visits I want to

The Rebel and Preacher Man

share. The first surprised me. I never met Russell's Assembly of God walking buddies although I knew of his confidence in their walk with the Lord. What a surprise when they stopped to visit me while I was in rehab at Parkview. Larry Parson and Steve Faxon came one day as I was having lunch outside my room, so they joined me. After a wonderful chat, they prayed heartwarming prayers for me and for Russell and our ministries. I cannot say enough about the love of God's family.

The second visitor came to visit the last week of my stay. Brock Lockhart was a senior in high school. He had surrendered to preach and been a faithful helper in children's camps. He absolutely glowed with the pure love of Jesus as he stopped by after school to express his concern for me, my health, and for Brother Russell. His precious hug and sincere prayer drew me right up to the Father's throne. Tremendous God hug! Amen!

56 - RESPITE THOUGHTS FROM MY JOURNALS

"To everything there is a season, A time for every purpose under heaven:"
Ecclesiastes 3:1 (KJV)

Various journal entries and thoughts gleaned from the forty days of my unplanned respite:

Day 1: Sunday, September 27

A young CNA brings me fresh water every morning with a smile, and "How are you today, dear? Can I bring you anything else this morning?" He looks like a shabby, grease monkey and moves like a nervous cricket, but he is the most tenderhearted, caring young man in this place. "Judge not..." Thanks, Lord!

Wednesday, October 7

Still on bi-pap and IVs and very, very sick, I am refreshed by the nurses and aides God allows me to witness to in my feeble way. At a very low time, a roommate encouraged me: "God will put you where you need to be. Trust Him and keep sharing your faith."

Saturday, October 10

I've been concerned about Russell; he is so worried. He assured me our kids have been calling or coming by every day to check on him. I am so proud of them and their families. Like most, they stay too busy. But they are there for us at a moment's notice. When I think how God blessed us with them, I am speechless. Thank You, God, for my family.

The Rebel and Preacher Man

Sunday, October 18

The room was packed, most of us in wheelchairs waiting for church. As the nurse started to turn on the TV (because no one came to lead) several people began to leave. With a sad heart and no ideas, I said, "I will do something if you want me to..." Before I could change my mind, she immediately wheeled me to the front and gathered the ones who had left. I continue to be amazed when God simply takes over. I felt such freedom. I told them a little bit about me and Preacher Man before I asked them for their favorite scriptures. Yes, I got "Jesus wept". We all laughed. I said it shows us Jesus was human, He understands when we weep. I asked them to hold their hands up if they needed prayer; then I prayed. We ended the short worship session by all singing "Jesus Loves Me". It was beautiful! I am in awe of the Presence of God; Lord, keep me pliable, a willing vessel.

Tuesday, October 20

I've had the same table partners all week. We three were wheeled to the table each day though now I can walk with a walker. Both ladies are quiet, frumpy, and non-communicative. Hard on me! But today a men's trio sang during our meal. My usually quiet tablemates were on the edge of their seats, all smiles; even singing their hearts out. Wow! Then, as the men left, one of the ladies threw a piece of her chicken at a lady across the room. Oh, Lord, remind me you see our hearts; help me to see and love their hearts, not their actions. And, Lord, please let me go home soon.

Thursday, October 27

I called my brother Richard on his 71st birthday.

"Sis, are they ever going to let you out of that place? Are you doing everything they tell you? Should I come help them?" My remarkable little brother!

October 27 - afternoon

Russell preached our dear friend, Ruby Chapman's funeral today. How I miss being there for him and with the family. Heaven's reunion is going to be grand someday. Thank you, Lord, I am still here; You are to be praised.

Friday, October 30, 2015, 6:30 AM

My eighty-eight-year-old roommate's request after her morning shower: "Let me have my jeans. No, no, not those. The other ones, and the blue shirt with flowers on the sleeves and collar, and those blue shoes that match." She made sure her makeup and hair were pristine before leaving the room for breakfast. In the meantime, seventy-two-year-old Susie (me) puts on one of her two pairs of black slacks, a tank top and one of her two shirts. No shoes and no makeup, but her hair is combed...sorta.

The hospital can't fix everything.

57 - PREACHER MAN PREPARES FOR A CHANGE

"For God is not unjust so as to overlook your work and the love that you have shown for his name in serving the saints, as you still do." Hebrews 6:10 (ESV)

Summer 2018

Summer had been the usual; visiting camps and Vacation Bible Schools, attending state conferences, spending time with the kids. We were busy yet thankful for the opportunity and health to continue serving the Lord.

As we sat on our back porch one evening, sipping our coffee, and watching the wildlife at play, Preacher Man caught me off guard.

"Susie, I've been thinking we should pray about retiring. We can still minister as God leads; I can preach, and you can continue with your ministries to the women. We both should slow down and spend more time together and with our families."

"What are you saying? Are you okay? Is there anything you should tell me? Are you going to resign as Director of Missions?"

"No, no. I haven't felt better in years. But I do think it's time for someone else to be Director of Missions. Not even Otis would believe I could have stayed this long. I have known for quite a while God was preparing a man to take my place."

Sitting together on our back porch, a soft breeze seemed to

whisper approval. We sipped our coffees and surveyed the peaceful Adams' Acres. God indeed blessed us with the perfect place to retire.

After that conversation, it seemed to me Preacher Man was becoming more intentional in his witnessing. Whether walking, shopping, or eating out, if there were people around, they were going to hear about his Jesus. He later told me God convicted him; he was to witness to every person he met.

As I look back on it now, I realize other changes gradually took place. Through the years, we took turns paying bills depending on which one could spare the time. Suddenly, it was important to him I did it all. "I've done it long enough, it's your turn."

He began to insist I be more focused on my writing: Get another "Patches" coloring book finished, start on our memoir, enter contests, and submit magazine articles. Not only did he congratulate me on the last contest I won, but he also mailed me a beautiful card. Above his signature, he wrote: "keep writing, the best is yet to come. I am proud of you."

> **AMAZING FACT:**
>
> The church Russell pastored when we met, Harmony Heights Baptist Church, was founded in 1960. What a year!! And what an amazing God we serve!

Director of Missions - DALLAS COUNTY - Missouri

As the seasons began to change, he gave me instructions on how to prepare the vehicles for winter. Each drive into town was an opportunity for him to point out the trustworthy mechanics. "I'm okay with you caring for the cars," I replied. He smiled and kept talking.

When we received the annual order form for a new DOM shirt from our state convention, I questioned ordering one. "Oh, yes, by all means send in an order. And keep the size as is; the new DOM will be needing it." Not only had he mentally made plans for his retirement year, he also had two people in mind to take his job.

"There are two preachers I think are ideal choices to lead our association when I step down. However, both are pastoring good churches. God has a plan; let's keep praying. I feel sure I know who God will choose to continue the work here. We will trust

God to stir his heart at the right time." Indeed, the one he prayed for followed him as Director of Missions of Dallas County Association of Southern Baptists. And, yes, his DOM shirts did fit quite nicely.

We began to put a few thoughts down for the memoir he wanted us to write. We both were aware our lives individually and collectively were flat out miracles from God. The fact was reinforced as we finally took time to talk about our growing up years.

Russell got teary-eyed when he mentioned his mother. He was the last child to leave home and clearly regretted not going home more often. He was convinced his salvation and ministry were the result of the prayers of his mother and his Itinerant Preacher Uncle, Rev. E.F. Adams. Both died before he was saved.

It was amazing to compare our lives in 1960. I was seventeen and graduated from Goodman High School. Russell was thirty-three years old and just accepted Jesus as his Savior and Lord. Three years later he surrendered to preach. Anxious to follow God, he quit his job at General Motors in Lockport, Illinois, only a few months before completing ten years at GM, and moved to Hannibal, Missouri, to begin preparing for the ministry.

So, now he was preparing to retire again. The next three years were the best of our ministry. It would take another book to write all the amazing works God did in and through His children as we, in our senior years, learned to focus more on Him and His plans for us.

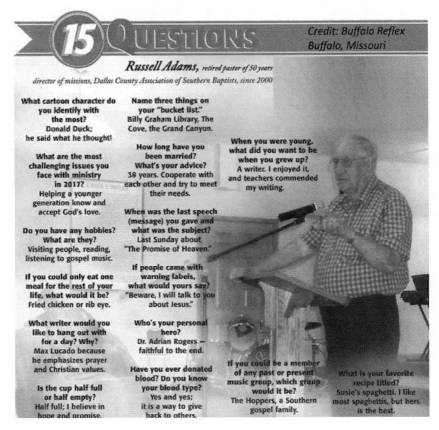

58 - MY ROMANTIC PREACHER MAN

"Rejoice in the Lord always. Again I will say rejoice!"
Philippians 4:4 (NKJV)

"What did Russell get you for your birthday? Or Christmas? Or...?"

"Nothing? He doesn't give you a gift on special days?"

In our forty plus years together, I have often been asked a similar question as friends and family show off their latest possession from the one they love. For all too many, I could sense the value they placed on the 'thing' they were given, and the hurt when the gift didn't measure up.

That is not me. And, thankfully, it was not Preacher Man either. Oh, don't get me wrong; he was unquestionably a gift giver. The most precious gifts he gave were those which could not be wrapped or explained to others.

Sometimes...many times, it was a tender touch and gentle hug when he could sense my world unraveling. If he questioned me at all, it was to ask how he could help. I knew by his presence; he was talking to our Father about me. I was in a place of safety until my storm blew over. Often his last words as we snuggled together in bed at night were, "I prayed for your day tomorrow. God will bless it."

Other times, it was an actual gift, though not necessarily on a particular holiday. Truthfully, without sounding too gooey here, I have to say he made every day special. Honestly, I do recognize I am a rebel, not the easiest to live with. But he loved me through the tough times and the good, and never questioned or tried to reform me.

I smile at his choice of flower planters. A bright blue car filled with daisies is in the bathroom. By my kitchen sink is a red truck planter resembling his red Ford Ranger; its flowers replaced with scouring pads. On my desk is a small vinyl recliner which actually reclines; the flower bin on the back is perfect for my pens and pencils. I have kept many more; these are valuable treasures that money cannot buy.

We did not exchange gifts or cards on every birthday or holiday. But, when either of us gave a gift, it meant something. He surprised me one day with a small, cuddly throw he saw at the grocery store. "I thought this pretty blanket would help you keep warm when we have our coffee on the back porch this fall." Priceless!

A gift I gave quite often was in saying "yes" when I wanted to say "no" to going with him to meetings, visits, or events. If I thought my saying "no" could have prevented him from going, or made him feel he needed to leave

early, I gladly accompanied him. It was important to me that he knew I supported him in whatever he was doing and wanted to be with him.

In the last years Mother was with us, I was unable to go to out-of-state conferences or revivals with him. On one occasion, after he packed his suitcase for a long trip, I sneaked into his suitcase and put stickers all over his things. On his socks: "Little socks, don't you take my guy to the wrong places!" On his toothpaste: "Let Jesus smile through you today," etc. I will forever remember picking him up at an airport. Dressed in his suit and tie, he was carrying his suitcase with brightly colored stickers all over the outside of it. He was not concerned about what others thought; because he wanted me to know he was proud of those stickers.

I have two stuffed animals I treasure. One is a colorful clown (I know-not actually an animal) from our first years together in Joplin, Missouri in the seventies. Shopping in Montgomery Wards store one evening, I spotted a clown in a bin of "stuff" out in the aisle. I did not know he watched me pick it up and put it down a few times. As we checked out our merchandise, he said, "Susie, you better go get your clown."

A second stuffed animal I enjoy cuddling is a big raccoon from Chapman's Furniture in Buffalo. When we bought our washer and dryer, I was enamored with this crazy animal's song about a Lazy Boy chair. I still squeeze his furry arm and close my eyes to remember Preacher Man's broad smile.

Every hillside in our Ozark Mountains is laden with beautiful trees. Why I claimed one tree near Springfield as "my tree" I'll never know. I have taken pictures of that tree in the rain, snow, high winds, with deer, with cows, with horses, loaded with leaves, barren, covered with webs, in a field of daisies, at sunrise and sunset. More than once, with no urging from me, Russell suggested we take a drive in hopes of capturing a unique photo of "my tree" in the changing weather. Do you know any guy in the world who would leave his recliner to drive his wife twenty-five miles through forests to take a picture of one single tree? That, sweet friend, is what you call a priceless gift!

When in St. Louis, Missouri, for our annual Missouri Baptist Convention one year, Russell was honored to bring the evening message at Arnold First Baptist Church. Dr. Adrian Rogers delivered the morning message. At the time, I was quite overweight and not as comfortable as I would have liked to have been. Russell's opening statement was the usual note of appreciation to the church. Then he said, "Do you see that lady in the third row in the pink shirt? That's my beautiful wife, Susie. You will want to meet her; she is God's gift to me." You cannot put a price on that!

Susie Kinslow Adams

Blessed Beyond Measure!
Survived 2020 - Trusting God for 2021

THANKFUL FOR FRIENDS AND FAMILY!
Blessed with 4 healthy kids, 5 grandkids, 8 greats.
(actually EACH ONE is great - GOD'S GIFTS TO US!)

Russell - turned 94 in June.
Walks every day, cheering folk along the way. Preaching/teaching more than the year before. Celebrates 20 years as Director of Missions where he keeps busy visiting the churches; faithfully encouraging and praying for the pastors. Helping others where he can; sharing joy to all. His greatest joy is sharing the Good News of Jesus Christ and leading many to know Jesus as their personal Lord and Savior.

Susie - turned 78 in December
"Thinks" of walking ... occassionally! Sends encouraging blog, cards, notes, texts. Working on 2 books; enters contests-wins some. Enjoys working with DCASB Women's Ministries and Office work. Thankful for a caring hubby that patiently takes her to clearance sales/closeouts keeping her goody bags filled and ready to share.

Together - we will celebrate 42 years in January.
We begin each day together; reading the Bible, praying, enjoying coffee and hot breakfast. Huddle in the kitchen for prayer before lunch; eat on the patio when weather's fitting. We enjoy serving Dallas County Association of Southern Baptists as a team. We carry bags of candy w/Scriptures and tiny Bibles to give as God directs. We relax by the fireplace with favorite movies and music, and counting our many blessings. We had work done outside and planted another 350 bulbs...hurry up springtime!

Merry Christmas! Happy New Year! Happy Valentines Day! Blessings on 2021!

Well, how has 2020 been for you and your family?
Blessed? Cursed? Happy? Sad? Challenging? Busy? Hectic? Broke? Unbelievable?

For us it has been a time to draw closer to the Lord and to each other. We're thankful for our warm, safe home with all the necessities of life (and more frills than we deserve!) Scriptures have taken on new meanings as our hearts ache for friends and family who have struggled through covid along with lockdowns and lost jobs. We have lost several close friends this year; many much younger than we.

We've learned to pray more fervently for each family member and friend by name. We ask God to stir the hearts of those who do not know Him personally; pleading for healing of soul and body for others and ourselves. *"Call to Me and I will answer you..."* Jeremiah 33:3 KJV We've clung to His promises; He remains faithful.

We have drawn closer to each other and our children and their families. At a time when one wondered who would be here at year's end, we learned to talk in a more personal way about current concerns and what the future holds. We talk of life, we talk of death, we talk of the future God has for each of us who trust Jesus as Savior and Lord. *"For I know the plans and thoughts that I have for you,' says the Lord, 'plans for peace and well-being and not for disaster, to give you a future and a hope."* Jeremiah 29:11 AMP. Thankful God has the final word!

We have learned to appreciate those who care for us and tend to our needs. Some people will not or cannot go out of their homes during this crisis. Yet, countless others faithfully serve us each day. The obvious: health care workers, first responders, transportation people, truckers that bring in food and supplies. Consider also mail carriers, trash haulers, grocers and their personnel, gas station attendants ... and on and on.

We're reminded each day what we have taken for granted. Simple, life-sustaining events have become illusive at best. We miss visiting in hospitals and nursing homes, shopping when and where we wish, hugging a friend in the store, planning a trip, dropping in on a neighbor. Worship online without opportunity to lift our voices together in song and prayer; and hug. We long to see unmasked smiles. We starve for hugs, laughter, freedoms. *"Teach us to number our days and recognize how few they are; help us to spend them as we should."* Psalm 90:12 TLB ..

From Isaiah 40 - *Comfort my people, says the Lord...they that wait upon the Lord shall renew their strength; they shall mount up with wings as eagles; they shall run, and not be weary; and they shall walk, and not faint.*
→ (WE COULD NOT KNOW— in EIGHT MONTHS, RUSSELL WOULD BE HOME WITH HIS JESUS!) ←
May God bless and keep you. May He make His face shine upon you and give you Peace.

What would I say to Preacher Man today?

"From the first day we met, you looked at me with that look I wasn't sure what to do with; you made me feel special and I wasn't sure why. By the end of the first week of knowing you, I was beginning to feel like I was the most beautiful woman God ever created by the way you treated me. I hadn't been looking for another man, I didn't want another man; but you weren't just another man! You always made time to listen to me, to pray with and for me. You taught me by example how to love and accept others; you made Jesus real to me.

You let me know every day how much you loved me. Not with diamonds and pearls or fancy things or trips. Not even with a dozen expensive roses. You let me know by a simple squeeze when I was nervous: By holding my hands and offering up a sincere prayer on my birthday: By a single tulip in a clear vase just because you thought of me.

And, though it was not what we desired, you prepared me as best you could for life without you. I will continue to follow your example and live my life to please Jesus alone until we meet again. I love you."

59 - MORE THAN A BUMP IN THE ROAD

"Peace I leave with you; my peace I give you. I do not give to you as the world gives. Do not let your hearts be troubled and do not be afraid." John 14:27 (NIV)

Summer 2021

The summer slowed us both down for a season. We had a bout with sciatica at the same time. Thankfully, it didn't last long, and Russell was ready to resume his daily "walk and talk" at Woods Grocery Store.

Then, the unexpected happened. Russell developed a painful blood clot in his right leg. Because of a concern about it moving to his lungs, he was taken by ambulance to Bolivar's Citizen's Memorial Hospital. As always, he left with a smile and a word for me. "Well, Susie, I hope I don't stay forty days like you did. I would sure miss your good cooking."

As I returned home from the hospital, I slowly coasted the car into the garage. Hands still on the steering wheel, I began to weep. For the first time, I thought of how terribly lonely it must have been for him to return home alone after my ambulance ride six years earlier.

Surely, this would not be a long stay for him. He was in excellent health except for this little clot. We were assured he should be back home in a few days.

Entering his room early the next morning, I felt like a teen in love. He beamed as usual and asked how my night had been; did I get good rest? He wanted to know how the kids were and who called. It seemed like a lot of chatter, even for him.

Sitting by his bed and holding hands, he opened the conversation he knew we needed to have.

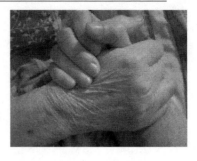

"The doctor was in early today. When they took the x-ray, they did not find a blood clot on my lungs; instead, they found a huge mass."

Time stood still as he allowed me to process the unexpected news.

"I don't think we have to know what it is, do you?"

We did not need a discussion on the option of further procedures or surgery at his age. My soulmate was tired; he had been ready to go home for a long time.

Later we could discuss his options and deal with the practical issues ahead of us. For now, we were left to sit in His Presence until the storm passed by.

He was in the hospital a few more days, then transferred to Buffalo Colonial Springs Health Care to regain strength before coming home. He was immediately put into hospice care; if they gave us a time frame, I don't remember. We were both familiar with hospice through our ministries and having several family members on hospice. Plus, Russell had served as Hospice Chaplain himself for twenty-five years.

At the time Russell talked of retirement, Cousin Penny developed serious health issues. Unable to manage her beautiful Branson home for herself, she hired 24-hour care; most of whom she neglected to have checked out before allowing them to move into her home.

After Earl died, she married, cared for, and buried two more husbands: Bud Schliesman and Dale Pritchard. Penny had taken care of people her entire life; Russell and I were hoping we could soon take care of her. We talked with her about moving to Buffalo.

She passed away about the time Russell was taken to Colonial Springs Health Care. As sad as this was for me, I could clearly see God's timing in all of it. With my husband in a facility with good care 24/7, I was free to spend time in Branson making her final arrangements and taking care of the necessary business at hand. It was bittersweet. I thanked God she was no longer in pain and turmoil, but what a hole she left in my life.

60 - A REASON FOR ALL THINGS

"For whosoever shall call on the name of the Lord shall be saved."
Romans 10:13 (KJV)

"Well, there has to be a reason God wants me to go to Colonial Springs." Preacher Man's every thought seemed to echo the same theme: what does God want me to do now?

He never questioned or discussed with me about hospice or being scheduled for therapy. Russell knew he was on mission; however long God gave him breath. He never had a cell phone or wanted one. In rehab, he asked a therapist to call me on her phone so we could chat while she did his therapy. Invariably, it sounded like a party. He knew he was on his way Home; nevertheless, he was enjoying life and wanted everyone included.

COVID-19 was rampant during this time and my visits were limited. I could go around to the back of the facility and see him through the window anytime. However, the rough terrain and heat of the day made it impossible for me to navigate. Instead, we talked on the phone as much as possible. Toward the end of his stay, there was one visit I simply had to make in person.

Back in July, writer Richard Nations interviewed Russell for an article he was doing for _The Pathway_, a Missouri Baptist Publication. Clearly, it was God's timing when the article was published on August 13. I needed to personally give him a copy, COVID or not! I'm thankful the facility worked with me; his excitement was well worth the struggle.

I can still see his smile and proud gleam in his eyes. "Look at this," he said. "I made the paper; a full page!" I left the copy with him; I am sure everyone in the place got to read it and hear him brag on Jesus.

(Read the article: https://mbcpathway.com/2021/08/13/missouris-oldest-dom-turns-95/)

The Rebel and Preacher Man

No one was surprised, including him, when he discovered the real reason he was there. One of the nurses working there came to his room with questions about the Lord. Before she left, she invited Jesus to come into her heart. God had Preacher Man there at the exact time needed to see one more person saved!

Michael, Ricky, and Debbie were all at Colonial Springs when it was time for their dad to come home. They formed quite a team as they worked together to get him and his paraphernalia transported.

He was very weak and unable to walk more than a few steps. Working together, they got him inside and settled down for a rest. It immediately felt like home with him in his recliner although we knew it would not be for long.

It was comforting to me to hear our children chat with their dad during his last few days. Ricky made a point to let Russell know how proud he was to call him "Dad". Debbie gave him his final shave. I can still hear her sweet comments, "Dad, you sure are a handsome fella. Yes, you are. I love you." Only God

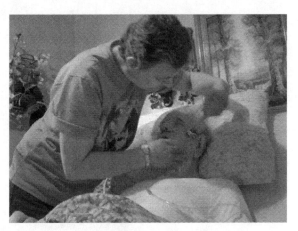

Debbie giving her dad a final shave

could have got Laura here from California at exactly the right time for her to say "good-bye" in the way she wanted to. Michael, too, spent some private time with his dad.

61 - PREACHER MAN'S HOMEGOING

"Even though I walk through the valley of the shadow of death, I will fear no evil, for you are with me; your rod and your staff, they comfort me." Psalm 23:4 (KJV)

There were many practical things to take care of and, surprisingly, some changes to make. Russell and I had planned to be buried in the Joplin area since it was our home base for so long.

"Mom, why are you taking him to Joplin when you live here? Your home is here." I don't recall which child said this, but I am thankful for the change.

Knowing our forty-two years of togetherness was ending, I stayed as close to him as I could. The first few days his voice was strong, and he wanted to visit with everyone. I can't begin to count the many pastors, friends, and neighbors who made short visits to pray with and support our family.

Not surprisingly, Russell knew exactly who he wanted to do his service. He chose men he respected; men he knew would share Jesus boldly as he did. He asked a friend from the Missouri Baptist Convention, Spencer Hutson, to do the graveside service. For the funeral service, he asked our pastor at Promise Point, Clifton Long, and Terry Gentry, Jr., pastor at Olive Point. Neither pastor expected his very blunt questions.

"Terry, are you a Christian?"

"Bro. Adams, you know I am a Christian."

"What makes you think so?" (Russell wanted to hear their testimonies.)

While it is hard to know the one you love is on their last lap, it's also a blessing to be able to say the things you want to say to them. On Russell's last day, I pulled a bench up close to him and

The Rebel and Preacher Man

held his hand with my left hand. With my right hand, I scribbled his answers to my questions, lest I forget.

He was very, very weak; his eyes barely open, his voice was soft and strained, but his grip on my hand was firm.

"Honey, is there anything particular you want at your service?"

He mentioned a few minor things and then, as if losing the energy to talk more, "You fix it like it needs to be. If you do it, I know it will be superb."

"I love you, Preacher Man."

"*I love you, too.*"

"I don't want you to go."

"*I don't want to go. But I have to go.*"

"I know, and it's okay."

He closed his eyes; I patted his hands and then went to the back porch.

"God, I don't like this! It's NOT okay!"

God sent our sweet friend, Chantel Carter as his hospice nurse. She was a patient helper and support as she stayed extra days to be with us until he was gone. Another medical friend, Donna Moriarty, happened to bring food and visit a minute at the time he was nearing the end. She felt honored to be with him when Jesus took him home.

As I recall, Rick and Michael seemed to take turns spending the night as his departure drew close. Debbie came every day. It was hard on her; she had been part of his family longer than any of us. She got to shave him and love on him his last few days. Laura and I sorted pictures for the mortuary display boards. Having her at home with me the following week was ideal for both of us.

All four kids helped me choose his burial plot. I am sure the caretaker wondered about us as we wandered around the cemetery. If I tried to describe our actions, few could understand. Certainly, we were brokenhearted; it was not a journey we wanted to take. Our lives were never going to be the same. But this gravesite would serve as a place to decorate in remembrance of a great husband, father, and grandfather. He is not there. He is Home in Heaven with his Jesus. That is a Precious Promise we can trust.

Even in times like these, there was so much for me to be thankful for. For forty-two years we shared a love story only God could pen. He entrusted us with four amazing children to love and care for, five GRAND grandchildren and a bunch of great grands.

Countless lives were changed forever through his plain preaching of God's love; souls were won to Jesus.

Marcella's brother, the Michael Williams family at Russell's funeral

62 - PERSONAL CHALLENGE FROM PASTOR RUSSELL ADAMS

"Finally, be strong in the Lord and in his mighty power. Put on the full armor of God, so that you can take your stand against the devil's schemes."
Ephesians 6:10-11 (NIV)

Three years before Russell was called home, God began stirring our hearts to write our story. From the beginning, we knew several of the chapters could be challenging. Simply writing our love story would be easy and fun. But God was asking us to do more.

His familiar words still ring in my ear: "I am sure God wants us to include the downside of ministry. There is no perfect church to be found; only Jesus is perfect. I am praying we will know exactly what God wants when the time is right. Susie, you and I know it was only by God's people praying for us that you and your mother even visited my church. All these years would never have happened if God had not put praying people in our lives.

We've been hurt by churches, mislead, and surprised by the actions of those we thought were strong Christian friends. Let's ask God to help us know exactly what He wants told."

***

A church is rightly defined as a body of baptized believers with Christ at the head. The church house, whatever its name, is only a building that houses The Church. Sadly, Christ is not always allowed to be the head of a congregation meeting inside a church house.

In one church, the very deacons Russell had ordained asked him to leave. Russell explained that God had called him there. "I cannot leave until God calls me away." It was not lack of opportunity to move that kept us there. He was offered several churches including a beautiful church out-of-state with a new, brick parsonage and extremely good benefits. God said, "Stay where you are." We did, and God blessed our family and ministries as only He could.

Church members who were determined to freeze the pastor out began withholding their tithes. Bills went unpaid and church repairs went unfinished. Not knowing why funds were low, an elderly couple gave the church $10,000 to take care of the church's needs. The only stipulation was... the pastor tell no one where the money came from, and he was to determine where to use it. The concerned couple also planned to will their home to the church for use as a parsonage. However, when they realized why there was a lack of funds, the couple changed their plans about the house.

When another church called for a vote on Preacher Man, a member said, "he only preaches salvation, and we are all saved. He needs to do more Bible teaching." The vote was not unanimous, but we stayed and had a fruitful ministry for quite a while before God moved us on.

Russell knew the Bible. He could quote more Scripture than I can remember. His messages were filled with biblical examples. His words from a note he left tell it best: "God didn't call me to be a Bible teacher. God called me to lead people to Christ. From the time I was saved, that one thing has motivated me. From street witnessing in Chicago door-to-door canvasing, to one-on-one encounters, I have only one message: you need Jesus, Jesus saves and Jesus alone."

If you are one of the many who are out of church because you have been hurt, your spirit crushed beyond belief,

The Rebel and Preacher Man

disillusioned by those who say they are Christians, please don't blame God. Those experiences, as difficult as they are, must not keep you from finding a group of dedicated believers to meet with regularly. God created us to need each other. WE NEED EACH OTHER.

Today's children and their families are continually bombarded by the world and its standards.

Do whatever it takes to get into God's Word; listen to radio or whatever device you have to hear Biblical teachers and preachers. Above all, pray. Ask God to put people in your path who are committed followers of Jesus.

My favorite pastor taught me to love and forgive and to look for the good in the worst of them. It was hard, the rebel in me wanted to fight back, retaliate, give them what they deserved for picking on my Preacher Man.

He gently reminded me of the grace God had given each of us. "Division and conflict is a heart problem. Only God can fix hearts. We cannot hate. We cannot be bitter. We must forgive. We must love as God loves us. We must pray for healing and restoration." His wise counsel is embedded in my heart. I will always love my "Preacher Man" and thank God for bringing us together because people like you prayed for a wife for him and a mother for his children. God hears our prayers!

63 - AT LAST, MY FINAL THOUGHTS

"For whether we live, we live unto the Lord; and whether we die, we die unto the Lord: whether we live therefore, or die, we are the Lord's." Romans 14:8 (KJV)

August 21, 2022

Our grandson, Rusty Adams, Mollie, and Jacklynn joined me in worship at Fair Play First Baptist Church. This was Russell's last pastorate before he "retired." It seemed right to celebrate his first year in heaven in this place.

It was a comforting time for me to worship with a congregation and pastor who remembered Preacher Man. Many remembered Rusty when he was a little lad visiting his grandpa's church. The hugs from old friends were warm and so welcome. God's family is awesome!

As you read our story, if your heart was stirred concerning your personal relationship with Jesus, do not take it lightly. Contact me. Call someone who knows Jesus.

Let's get this settled. There is not one thing more important in all the world than to know that you know that you know....

***

The rebel in jail in chapter one was a terrified teen, far from home and those she loved. The over-dramatic officer who tossed her into jail could well have been Barney Fife. He had no legal right whatsoever to lock her up. Going door-to-door selling books without a permit was never considered a jailable offense. Had it been so, it was her manager who should have been the one in jail, not her.

This incident may or may not have been my only jail experience. The plain truth of the matter is that a loving God allowed a sassy, energetic officer to put the fear of prison into a

The Rebel and Preacher Man

vulnerable teen. At a time when God was the farthest thought from my mind, He was a faithful Heavenly Father guiding and protecting His child.

When I take my last breath, I will still be telling how a miracle-working God poured His love and mercy into a country girl with a rebel spirit and a farm boy old enough to be her dad. Through His grace alone, we were given forty-two years together to raise four remarkable children.

As perhaps with some of you, I have been asked what I would change about my life decisions. What would I do over? Would I knuckle down in school and work to my full potential? Would I lose the five pounds and join the Navy instead of traipsing across the country? At eighteen would I reconsider marrying a guy I knew nothing about? Would I take a little boy to raise when I still needed raising myself? Would I marry a preacher I just met?

Or –would I do it all over again the exact same way? And my answer to the last question would be: Oh, yes, yes, yes! A thousand times yes!

God never wastes anything. God has made something beautiful from all my messes. I plead with you - trust God with your messes; He alone can make them into something beautiful.

Volumes could not contain the stories of lives changed and people brought to a saving knowledge of Jesus as we made a point to love those He put in our paths. God longs to use every one of His children in that way regardless of age, past or current circumstance in life.

As a teen I desperately needed to learn to let go and let God. I need the reminder still. Any child of God can tell you, the more we learn to love Him, the more He will love on others through us.

REMEMBERING RUSSELL ADAMS

At 82, serving as Director of Missions for Mid Missouri Baptist Association, I wondered if I wasn't already too old for the job, but then I met Russell, 87, going strong with no thought of retiring or quitting! From the beginning he was an inspiration to me and, I believe, every one of our DOMs. He was the oldest DOM in our state and maybe in the entire SBC! I called him for some advice regarding duties of this position. He not only gave me good counsel, but also sent a large packet of helpful information. Lord, give us more like Russell Adams!
~Larry Lewis, former Director of Missions, former president of the Home Mission Board, and former President of Hannibal-LaGrange University.

On my way to do an estimate in town, I remember driving by Pastor Russell as he was out for a walk. He did not see me, but, when he reached the stop sign, he grabbed it and swung around. The "Joy of the Lord" in his heart was shared to me in that moment; I do cherish that memory. There is a lot to be said for staying ' young at heart'!
~Chuck and Marsha Hinaman, Majestic Builders, Rohnert Park, California

Brother Adams was my pastor at Harmony Heights when I was saved and baptized in 1979. I still have the Bible with his signature in it and the church covenant bookmark he handed out explaining our beliefs. As a young girl, I thought of Bro. Adams as a "gentle giant" because he looked huge to me in stature but was so kind and caring and gentle to those around him ~Michele Walters Snider

Brother Adams was our pastor when I was saved. After we prayed together, he told me that before I did anything else, I should go and tell my mom right then. I did just what he told me to do. I will always be thankful for the fact that Bro. Adams was our pastor when I was a child. ~Tanya Walters Tatro

Russell was a good and caring pastor. His messages were always plain and simple from the Bible so all could understand the plan of salvation. There was a time when the Cooperative Program was being criticized for its use of funds. When I asked Russell about my concerns, his reply was, "It's the best plan I know of for spreading the gospel and supporting our missionaries. Until the Lord shows me a better plan, I will continue to support it."
~Betty Dunfee, Dunfee Funeral Home, Grant City, Missouri

Preacher Boy Class given by Russell Adams led me into supply preaching. His leadership and training gave me the confidence to preach the Gospel of Jesus Christ. When I faced an issue, I went straight to Russell; his calm demeanor brought sense to the situation. He helped me handle things to a good outcome. He was always a great encourager and full of knowledge and the love of Christ. I count him as one of the Godliest men I've ever known.

~Bud Riley

Russell,

I want to be like you when I grow up!

Hosea Bilyeu

Hosea Bilyeu, Pastor, Author, Musician, County Commissioner

I am so very sorry for your loss. He was such a wonderful man. I have known him for over 50 years, ever since he was at Grant City FBC. I loved our times together at DOM retreat. He loved the Lord and was always sharing about Jesus! I love you and am praying for you. ~Jean Brown

Church with Jesus!!! Can't get any better! ~Enid Rauh Kelsay

I will always remember Russell as a mentor for believers. He taught me to be patient and wait upon the Lord for guidance and direction. We all will miss him here on this earth but a heavenly reunion will be coming soon. ~Jack Trombley

Heaven's gain is surely a big loss for you, Susie. I'm glad Bob and I got to meet Russell and spend some time with him.
~Brenda Poinsett

Prayers of comfort from Jim and I. Russell is now experiencing exactly what he has preached all those years. ~Sharon Chilton

Makes me sad… he's had a major impact on me since I was little. One of the best men I've ever known!!!
~Justin Wingo

I can't ever repay Russell and Susie for the blessings they have been in my life, my family's life. Russell got me back in church by his preaching. I heard him a few times in my early years and didn't want to listen to him-stubborn, I know! Then came back and it all clicked and now I am very involved in my church. He helped lead my soon-to-be husband to the Lord one night on his porch. I had wanted my husband to be saved before we married; God provided this through Russell. He and Susie prayed with me and my new-born son; there was no greater joy for me than in that moment to be with them as we neared a scary operation for our son. Russell was nearing the end of his own life and still cared enough to want to save souls and helped lead my sister to the Lord one day. Both Russell and Susie were/are a great blessing for us. ~Chelsey Ownby

FINAL THOUGHT:

In reading some of my precious husband's personal notes, I found this prayer he had written in April, 2012, at age 86. God graciously answered his prayer in the nine years that followed. –
Susie Adams

"Dear Father, my prayer to you today is you will cleanse me and make of me a better servant to be used in the work of Your Kingdom. Give me special opportunities to witness. Amen."

PASTORATES OF REV. RUSSELL A. ADAMS

1964-1967	Southside Baptist - Vandalia, MO
1967-1970	First Baptist Church - Ewing, MO
1970-1973	Grant City Baptist - Grant City, MO
1974-1977	Northeast Baptist - Clinton, MO
1977-1982	Harmony Heights Baptist - Joplin, MO
1982-1985	Southern Hills Baptist - Miami, OK
1986-1991	Lakeview Baptist - Lakeview, CA
1991-1996	First Baptist Church - Rohnert Park, CA
1996-2000	First Baptist Church - Fair Play, MO
2000-2021	Director of Missions - Dallas County Association Southern Baptist - Buffalo, MO

Listen to the last sermon Rev. Adams spoke at age 95: "Why I Became a Christian"

Russell Adams - Age 95 Why I became a Christian

https://www.youtube.com/watch?v=5KeEKx1vcRc

ABOUT THE AUTHOR

Susie Kinslow Adams is a gifted and award-winning author, writer, speaker and storyteller. She worked alongside her husband, Dr. Russell Adams, as he pastored churches and served as Director of Missions for Dallas County Association of Southern Baptists. Susie led in women's Bible studies and directed women's retreats in California, Oklahoma, and Missouri.

An active member of Springfield Writer's Guild and American Christian Writers, Susie has won many writing contests. Her books: <u>My Mother My Child,</u> (a practical guide and workbook on dealing with Alzheimer's), and two children's activity books, <u>Patches' Joyland Express,</u> and <u>Patches' Farmland Adventures</u> are available on Amazon. Another children's activity book is planned for release in 2024.

More information and informative articles are available at www.susiekinslowadams.com. Sign up for her encouraging blog and receive a free cookbook.

THANK YOU

Thank you for reading *The Rebel and Preacher Man*. I hope you were blessed and encouraged, or inspired to tell someone else about it! I would be so pleased if you left a kind review.

ಅಶಃ

If you enjoyed this true love story, you might enjoy *My Mother, My Child*. This easy-to-read, very personal book will help and encourage you whether you are: An adult caring for aging parents The parent of small children A professional caregiver An individual wanting to help others. Read how the author finds joy in the complex, daily demands of a caregiver. Realize you are not in this alone as you learn where and how to find help. The thought-provoking questions and insights at the end of each chapter are suitable for individual or group study. No two situations are the same, however, the basic responsibilities and standard of care will not change. Every person is entitled to adequate care and respect regardless of age or circumstance.

Order it here in print or digital format.

ಅಶಃ

Made in the USA
Columbia, SC
10 February 2024

fdb4fc37-73b1-4c86-836d-2eb03d5d8359R01